Anti-Inflammatory Diet
Instant Pot Cookbook

The Only Anti-inflammatory Diet Recipe Cookbook In 2018 For Your Instant Pot Cooking To Decrease Inflammation, Be More Healthier And Longevity

Teresa Frank

© **Copyright 2018 -Teresa Frank -All rights reserved.**

In no way is it legal to reproduce, duplicate, or transmit any part of this document by either electronic means or in printed format. Recording of this publication is strictly prohibited, and any storage of this material is not allowed unless with written permission from the publisher. All rights reserved.

Legal Notice:
This book is copyright protected. This is only for personal use. You cannot amend, distribute, sell, use, quote or paraphrase any part or the content within this book without the consent of the author or copyright owner. Legal action will be pursued if this is breached.

Disclaimer Notice:
Please note the information contained within this document is for educational and entertainment purposes only. Every attempt has been made to provide accurate, up to date and reliable, complete information. No warranties of any kind are expressed or implied. Readers acknowledge that the author is not engaging in the rendering of legal, financial, medical or professional advice.
By reading this document, the reader agrees that under no circumstances are we responsible for any losses, direct or indirect, which are incurred as a result of the use of information contained within this document, including, but not limited to, —errors, omissions, or inaccuracies.

Table of Contents

Introduction 11

Chapter 1: Everything About Chronic Inflammation 12

    What is Inflammation? 12

    What causes Inflammation? 12

        Diet 13

        Aging 14

        Obesity and Inactivity 14

        Sleep Deprivation 14

        Stress 15

        Sun Exposure 15

        Smoking 15

    Craze Behind Inflammation 15

    Science of Inflammation 16

    Harmful side effects of Inflammation 18

    Different symptoms of Inflammation 19

    About Anti-Inflammatory Diet 19

    Great Tips For Anti-Inflammatory Success 20

    Foods Good For Anti-Inflammatory Diet 20

    Foods Bad For Anti-Inflammatory Diet 21

    Frequently Asked Questions 22

        1. Should I Detox Before Anti-Inflammation? 22

        2. Should I See A Doctor For My Inflammation? 22

        3. Should I Exercise More? 22

Chapter 2: All About The Instant Pot 23

    What is an Instant Pot? 23

    Anatomy of the Instant Pot 23

    Understanding the buttons of Instant Pot 24

Crucial components of Instant Pot..26

Advantages of using Instant Pot...27

Using Instant Pot...28

Cooking Guidelines...28

    Cook timetable: Fruits..29

    Cook timetable: Vegetables..29

    Cook timetable: Rice and Grains...32

    Cook timetable: Fish and Seafood..33

    Cook timetable: Beef, Chicken, Turkey..33

    Cook timetable: Beans, Legumes, Lentils..35

Instant Pot buying guide...36

    IP-DUO60..36

    IP-DUO Plus60...37

    IP-DUO80..38

    IP-ULTRA..38

    IP-Smart Bluetooth..39

    IP-LUX60 V3...40

Chapter 3: Vegan And Vegetarian..41

Mashed Cauliflower..41

Cauliflower Rice..41

Brussel Sprouts...42

Baked Potato...43

Squash Spaghetti and Garlic Sage..43

Garlic Mashed Potatoes..44

Pickled Chilies...44

Zucchini Pasta Pesto..45

Mexican Pinto Bean...46

Stuffed Acorn Squash..46

Mashed Vegetable Platter	47
Potato And Beans	48
Lentil and Millet	49
Refried Beans	49
Eggplant Spread	50
Indian Dal	51
Artichokes	51
Vegan Pasta Sauce	52
8 Vegetable Stir Fry	53
Cabbage Rice	53
Black-Eyed Peas	54
Pindi Chole	55
Vegetable Gumbo	56
Eggplant Sambar	56
Smokey Gouda Sauce	57
Daal Makhani	58
Spinach And Potatoes	59
Lentil Bolognese	59
Picatta Potatoes	60
Mushroom and Green Pea Curry	61
Gourd Curry	61
Marinara Sauce	62
Garlic and Broccoli Mishmash	63
Parsnip And Potato Mash	63
Garlic Potatoes	64
Millet Pilaf	64
Spicy Cauliflower	65

Vegan Dumplings..66

Vegan Shepherd's Pie..66

Chapter 4: Grains...68

Healthy Oatmeal...68

Cinnamon Oatmeal..68

Berry Oatmeal...69

Peach Oatmeal..70

Veggie Risotto...70

Asian Styled Quinoa..71

Mushroom Risotto...71

Steel Cut Oats...72

Biryani..72

Butternut Squash Risotto...73

Irish Oatmeal..74

Melba and Peach Oatmeal..75

Porridge..75

Millet Porridge..76

Red Lentil Rice..76

Confetti Basmati Rice..77

Jasmine Rice...78

Coconut Rice...78

Polenta Bites...79

Spicy Pickled Green Chili...79

Curried Mushrooms..80

Spicy Roasted Potatoes...81

Chapter 5: Soups and Stews..82

Onion Soup...82

Lentil Soup..82

Butternut Squash Soup..83

Cream of Carrot Soup..84

Cream of Pumpkin Soup..84

Cream of Celery Soup..85

Apple and Broccoli Soup...86

Black-Eyed Peas Hummus...86

Cream of Potato and Celery Soup..87

Spiced Quinoa..88

Mushroom and Barley Bowl..88

Potato and Chard..89

Egg Bowl Soup..90

Pumpkin Curry Soup..90

Tomato Basil Soup...91

Bean Chili..92

Vegetable Lentil Soup..92

White Onion And Carrot Soup..93

Smoky Split Pea Soup...94

Bean Stew..94

Cauliflower And Sweet Potato Soup...95

Bean Chili..96

Leafy Greens Soup..96

Coconut and Tomato Soup..97

Vegetable Stock...98

Curry Dal Makhani..99

Cream of Mushroom Soup..99

Black Bean Soup...100

Beet Borscht...101

Fennel And Cauliflower Soup...102

Chapter 6: Drinks and Smoothies...103

Mango And Ginger Infused Water..103

White Hot Chocolate..103

Peach And Raspberry Lemonade...104

Hot Apple Cider...104

Blueberry Lime Juice..105

Sweet Cranberry Juice..105

Hot Peppermint Vanilla Latte..106

Berry Shrub...106

Cooked Iced Tea...107

Hibiscus Tea..107

Apple Cinnamon Water..108

Wassail..109

Instant Horchata...109

Jamaican Hibiscus Tea..110

Ginger Ale..110

Blackberry Italian Drink..111

Chapter 7: Sauces..112

Bone Broth..112

Vegetable Broth...112

Worcestershire Sauce...113

Red Hot Sauce...114

Chapter 8: Seafood..115

Tuna Zoodles..115

Salmon And Vegetables...115

Chili Salmon.. 116

Orange and Salmon.. 117

Swordfish... 117

Fried Salmon Patties.. 118

Curry Tilapia.. 118

Coconut Curry Fish.. 119

Cod.. 120

Sock Eye Salmon... 120

Bowl Of Shrimp... 121

Shrimp Chowder... 121

Lemon Pepper Salmon... 122

Shrimp Rice... 123

Lobster Bisque... 124

Country Shrimp... 125

Seafood Gumbo... 125

Garlic Mussels... 126

Seafood Stew.. 127

Chapter 9: Salads...128

Beet Salad... 128

Kale and Carrots Medley... 128

Vegetable Salad... 129

Capers And Beet Salad... 130

Couscous And Vegetable Medley.. 130

Stir Fried Bell Pepper and Potatoes... 131

Lentil and Farro Salad.. 132

Peruvian Quinoa... 132

English Peas And Asparagus... 133

Cauliflower Citrus Salad..134

Egg and Olive Potato Salad...134

Sweet Pickle Potato Salad..135

Quinoa Salad...136

Chapter 10: Dessert..137

Apple Sauce...137

Mango Sticky Rice..137

Apple Bake..138

Apple Cranberry...138

Carrot Puree...139

Cranberry Sauce..139

Gaja Ka Halwa (Pudding - India)...140

Conclusion...141

Introduction

Dear readers, this is Teresa Frank. At first, I'd like to thank you for purchasing this book and supporting me in my journey. Hope this book will do good to you! Before we reading this book, please let me ask you some questions:

Do you have an Instant Pot or wanna have one? Do you want to be professional about instant pot using and have delicious foods? **Do you often have chronic inflammation?** Do you often feel uncomfortable but have no idea about the reason? **Do you want to solve these problems and be more longevity?** If yes for any of above questions, then this book is for you!

With more than 43 million people suffering from arthritis, and another 25 million suffering from Asthma in the US alone, inflammation is a condition at an all-time high and near to becoming an epidemic. With that in mind, it is not unusual that Americans are trying to find ways to alter their lifestyle and decrease inflammation. That is what I plan to achieve with this book.

Not only we will give you the answer of Anti-inflammary Diet, but also we have provided you with most useful information about Instant Pot cooking, which allows you to save an immense amount of time while lowering down your Inflammatory effects! This book acts as a one stop guide for you to fully understand the concepts of both the Instant Pot and the Anti-Inflammatory diet. Meantime we have provided **150+** easy to understand recipes, all to help you master your cooker and create very own masterpiece.

Inside this book, you will find: **Vegan & Vegetarian, Grains, Soups, Broth and Stews, Smoothies, Drinks and Brunch, Seafood, Salad, and Desserts recipes**. All recipes do good to your health and and will decrease inflammation. They are well-chosen and chef-proved, easy to follow recipes. All recipes have detailed procedure, which lead you easy to make all of these delicious recipes! Now all you need to do is following this book. Take action!

Chapter 1: Everything About Chronic Inflammation

This chapter will be dedicated to providing the fundamental concept of chronic inflammation, and how your diet can alleviate some or all of the issue. Let's start off with the most basic question first.

What is Inflammation?

In the most basic definition, inflammation is the process of the body's white cells and their accompanying substances trying to protect the body from infection due to foreign body contamination, such as virus or bacteria.

It all sounds good, right?

However, in certain diseases such as arthritis, the defense mechanism seems to malfunction and the immune system tends to trigger an inflammatory response, even when there are no foreign invaders in the body.

Diseases that tend to do these are largely known as "auto immune" diseases and instead of protecting the body, the body's own auto immune system starts to harm itself and damage tissue.

What causes Inflammation?

Various factors come into play when considering the reasons as to "what" causes inflammation in a human being. More often than not, a vast majority of the reasons are linked to poor lifestyle choices, however, it should be noted that aging is also a factor.

Some of the most crucial causes include:

Diet

If we make a comparison, we would soon see that most of the causes of Inflammation are related to diet, so we are keeping this at the top of the list.

Harmful substances such as refined fats, animal products, and refined carbohydrates cause damage in the long run.

It should be noted though that carbohydrates don't directly contribute to inflammation, but refined foods with higher concentration and fats are found to be naturally dense with inflammation-causing substances that affect the gut and increases inflammation.

The types of fat consumed by an individual also play a role here. Back in the early days when everything was simple, people used to stay on a diet that was well-balanced on both Omega-3 and Omega-6 fats. However, modern diets tend to have a high concentration of Omega-6 fat as oppose to the Omega-3 fat, this increases the possibility of suffering from inflammation by 10-20%.

It is important for the body to have a good supply of Omega-3 fatty acids because the Omega-6 and Omega-3, both compete for the same COX enzymes, which are needed to build large fatty molecules.

COX-2 enzyme in particular is essential for making inflammatory prostaglandins.

Too much Omega-6 fatty acids will result in the domination of this enzyme and the body won't be able to utilize the enzyme anymore in conjunction with Omega-3 fats to reduce inflammation.

Nowadays fats are chemically modified and this plays a greater role to inflammation as well. They are made to be more inexpensive, which results in the production of highly inflammatory products.

Aging

The natural process of aging contributes to inflammation as well. As we age, the body's cells can regenerate but most of them start to die, leaving behind waste material that can trigger inflammation.

Obesity and Inactivity

Excessive inactivity can and will often lead to obesity, which is a major cause of inflammation.

Adipose tissue, the layer of fat that is found right under our skin is actually responsible for much more than just keeping it warm.

It is a metabolically active layer that causes the body to change the body chemistry and is also affected by the body's other systems.

The fat layer contains a large number of white blood cells and greater level of fat.

The cell count is linked together. Meaning, the more fat there is, the greater number of white cells will be present.

These cells often release pro-inflammatory substances that gradually contribute to the rise of inflammatory effects.

Sleep Deprivation

Researchers have shown that a lack of sleep is linked to the formation of certain infection-fighting white blood cells such as T-Cells. Depriving ourselves of sleep will cause the number of T-Cells to decrease, which in turn increase the number of inflammation-promoting cytokines.

Stress

Cortisol is a hormone produced by adrenal glands and used to manage the body's response to stress.

It helps stimulate bursts of energy and suppresses pro-inflammatory substance.

This also helps to reduce stress by counter-acting the effects of pro-inflammatory eicosanoids. However, if you stress too much, the amount of cortisol might increase to a dramatic level that will cause your immune cells to lose sensitivity to this hormone and trigger inflammation.

Sun Exposure

This might seem a little bit surprising, but excessive exposure to sunlight can often result in an individual suffering from inflammation.

Sunburn or over-exposure encourages the formation of free radicals under the skin surface. Just to let you know, free radicals are unstable molecules that tend to destroy injury-fighting cells and lower the number of white blood cells present in the body.

As you may have guessed, this lowers the strength of the body's immune system and leads to inflammatory attacks.

Smoking

Exposure to various toxins such as cigarette smoke plays a high role in inflammation. Either second hand or first hand, inhaled tobacco tend to cripple the body's capacity to fight diseases by suppressing the production of white blood cells.

Craze Behind Inflammation

So, why are people heading for an anti-inflammatory diet?

Despite having the best technology and health care services in the world, America is still suffering from an epidemic of chronic inflammation and other chronic inflammatory diseases.

The change in the form of modern diet is contributing to increasing the number of incidents as well.

When we are referring to chronic inflammation, we are implying various diseases such as arthritis, asthma among the long-term illnesses/diseases.

As stated at the beginning of the chapter, In the US alone, nearly 43 million people suffer from arthritis and 25 million suffer from Asthma.

Those are no small numbers, and the need for Americans to find a proper solution for the anti-inflammatory regime is at all-time high.

Science of Inflammation

Now that you have a little idea of just how severe of a problem inflammation is, let us have a look at how inflammation works, and what happens to your body during inflammation.

When your body needs to respond to an injury, it tends to mobilize an army of specialized cells to fend of the invading organism and toxins.

These cells prepare pathways for fighter cells to attack and completely engulf the attackers.

Once that has happened, another group of cells tend to signal to the body and let it know the fighter cells have accomplished their task and the body is allowed to stop the production of preparatory and fighter cells.

These results a sort of cleanup that clears up the leftover fighter cells from the battlefield and repairs any damage.

Simply put, there are two steps to this response:

- Pro-Inflammatory

- Anti-Inflammatory

Each cell involved in the pro stage builds on the work of the previous cells and helps to make the immune reaction stronger for any upcoming attack.

During pro period, symptoms such as redness, swelling, itching are common.

The anti-inflammatory is the reverse of pro-inflammatory and it works to lower the effects of inflammation.

A variety of substances used to block inflammation are made from essential fatty acids, which the body isn't able to produce on its own.

These acids must be obtained through supplements or foods.

Two essential ones are Omega-3 and Omega-6.

Omega-6 tend to increase inflammation while Omega-3 helps to reduce it.

It should be noted that what I wrote above is a simplified version of the whole mechanism and there is a lot more to it.

There are various substances that play a deeper role in the whole infrastructure that allows the body to control its inflammatory mechanism.

Some of the crucial ones are:

- **Histamine:** White blood cells near an injury tend to release a substance known as histamine. They increase the permeability of blood vessels around the wound that signals fighter cells and other substances to regulate an immune response and come to the sight of injury. Histamine also causes redness and swelling around the affected region and causes runny nose, rash, itchy eyes.
- **Cytokines:** These are proteins that are activated by pro-inflammatory eicosanoids to signal fighter cells to gather at the injury site. They are responsible for diverting energy from the body to catalyst the healing process. Release of these substance tend to cause tiredness and decrease appetite.
- **C-Reactive Protein:** Cytokines alongside other pro-inflammatory eicosanoids are closely involved in the activation of a substance known as

C-Reactive Protein. This particular organic compound produced by the liver responds to messages that are sent out by white blood cells. The C-Reactive proteins tend to bind the site of injury and act as a sort of surveillance unit that helps to identify the invading bodies.
- **Leukocytes:** Several types of leukocytes (also known as white blood cells) are critical to the process of neutralizing invading substance. Neutrophils, for example, are small, agile and are able to first arrive at the scene of crime to ingest small microbes. However, large substances such as macrophages as required to tackle a large number of microbes.

There are a few more, but the gist still remains the same. When your body starts to suffer from an uncontrolled inflammation attack, the action of these and similar substances tend to get out of control, which results in extremely uncomfortable situations.

Harmful side effects of Inflammation

Uncontrolled inflammation results in diseases that are known as autoimmune diseases. While there are a large number of them out there, some of the more prominent ones are:

- **Type 1 Diabetes:** Type 1 Diabetes can cause the immune system to attack and destroy insulin producing cells in your pancreas that disrupt the regulation of sugar levels in your body.
- **Rheumatoid Arthritis:** RA causes the immune system to attack certain joints that can result in discomfort and pain.
- **Psoriatic Arthritis:** This causes skin cells to multiply rapidly, which results in red and scaly patches on your skin called plaques.
- **Multiple Sclerosis:** MS tends to damage the protective coating that surrounds nerve cells (known as myelin sheath) and affect the transmission of neural messages between the brain and body. This leads to weakness, balance issues, along with other symptoms.
- **Inflammatory Bowel Syndromes:** This disease causes irritation of the intestinal lining.
- **Graves' Disease:** This disease attacks the thyroid gland in your neck and causes it to overproduce hormones, which results in an imbalance.

- **Cancer:** Cancerous tumors tend to secret substances cytokines and free radicals that cause inflammation, which tumors growing. If you already suffer from inflammation, it c the situation words.
- **Alzheimer's:** The brain does not have pain receptors, but that mean it won't be able to feel the effects of inflammation. Resear have recently discovered that people with a high level of Omega-6 f acids tend to have a greater chance of developing Alzheimer's.

Different symptoms of Inflammation

While there are different types of diseases that are caused by Inflammation, the early symptoms of them are similar. These include:

- Fatigue
- Muscle ache
- Low-grade fever
- Redness and swelling
- Numbness in your feet and hands
- Loss of hair
- Skin rash

These are often accompanied by the symptoms that are specific to any disease the patient might be suffering from.

About Anti-Inflammatory Diet

Generally speaking, an anti-inflammatory diet consists of a diet comprised of foods targeted towards the reduction of uncontrolled inflammatory response in the body.

Anti-inflammatory diet is rich in foods packed with anti-oxidants that are reactive molecules in food to help to reduce free radicals, which causes cell damage to the body.

...popular diets already following the anti-inflammatory ...[Medi]terranean diet which is comprised of fish, good fats, and...

...-Inflammatory Success

...ing a complete anti-inflammatory diet, the following steps ...further up the ante and improve your condition:

- ...at a wide variety of fruits and vegetables of different colors
- Reduce the amount of junk food you consume
- Eliminate sugary beverages and sodas from your diet
- Create healthy shopping lists; avoids buying unhealthy items
- Carry anti-inflammatory snacks while you are on the go
- Drink water
- Maintain a healthy calorie intake
- Try including Omega-3 supplements and turmeric in your diet
- Exercise on a regular basis
- Make sure to get proper sleep

These will help you to significantly accelerate your progress.

Foods Good For Anti-Inflammatory Diet

Despite popular belief, following an anti-inflammatory diet isn't difficult. The following foods will encourage a healthy anti-inflammatory lifestyle:

- Dark leafy greens such as kale and spinach
- Blueberries, cherries, black berries
- Dark red grapes
- Cauliflower and broccoli
- Green tea
- Beans and lentils
- Red wine (in moderation)
- Avocado and coconut

- Olives
- Extra virgin olive oil
- Walnuts, almonds, pistachio, pine nuts
- Cold water fish; salmon and sardines
- Spices and herbs; cinnamon , turmeric
- Dark chocolate
- Watermelon
- Onion
- Whole grains; brown rice, bulgur, quinoa
- Eggs
- Tomatoes

These are just the basics, there are a lot more to look out for.

Foods Bad For Anti-Inflammatory Diet

Foods you should avoid if you want to keep your inflammation in check.

- Sugary foods; soda, baked sweets, candy, sweetened coffee
- Vegetable oil products; mayonnaise, BBQ sauce, potato chips, crackers
- Fried foods; french fries, fish sticks, fried chicken, onion rings
- Refined flour products; pizza, pasta, flour tortillas, bagels, crackers
- Dairy; milk, yogurt, butter, soft cheeses
- Artificial sweeteners; means no-sugar added products such as diet coke
- Artificial additives; including breakfast cereals, ice cream, candy
- Saturated fats; burgers, chips, pizza, and candy
- Conventional grain-fed meats; beef, pork, chicken
- Processed meats; bacon, sausage, jerk, hot dogs
- Gluten from store bought products; bread, white flour
- Alcohol in excess
- Trans food fats; margarine, baked goods such as cookies, doughnuts, muffins
- Fast food

ked Questions

re Anti-Inflammation?
r body, you are essentially flushing out the harmful
 in your body.

re embarking on your anti-inflammation is an
suring the effectiveness of your new lifestyle.

d I See A Doctor For My Inflammation?
 anti-inflammation lifestyle is a regime largely based on vegetables and requires an individual to omit certain products such as dairy products and red meat. If you are already following a similar kind of diet; such as vegan, then you would have less issue changing your eating habits.

However, if you are taking such a step for the first time and trying to completely shift your lifestyle, it is recommended you consult a physician to ascertain you are in a healthy place to change your eating habits.

Alternatively, if you are already suffering from an auto-immune disease then it is even more advised to consult with your doctor in order to create a meal plan according to your requirements.

3. Should I Exercise More?
Having a fit and healthy body definitely helps reduce the possibility of experiencing issues when you begin this new lifestyle. If you are obese, you may face some inflammatory reactions, so it is better to start with a minimum level of exercise in your day-to-day routine before progressing to more strenuous exercising.

Chapter 2: All About The Instant Pot

With the basics of anti-inflammatory diet out of the way, let's have a look at the instant pot.

What is an Instant Pot?

To keep things short and to the point, the instant pot is a very versatile cooking device that is able to properly cook delicious meals by utilizing the power of high pressure cooking.

A general idea is to think of the device as being the evolutionary peak form of electric pressure cookers.

However, to better understand how the instant pot works, you should understand the meaning of the term pressure cooking.

So, in layman's terms, pressure cooking is the process of cooking a meal inside a sealed vessel by trapping or generating steam inside the device.

As for the "how?"

Simply put, the boiling point of water increases as the pressure increases.

When considering the instant pot, steam is generated inside, the pressure increases, which allows water to reach high temperature without actually being boiled. This helps to significantly reduce the time taken to prepare meals. Especially when compared with other traditional cooking methods.

Anatomy of the Instant Pot

Keep in mind that different manufacturers will try to include something "special" to make their device unique. However, the following are staple to every electric pressure cooker, including the instant pot.

- A cooker will have an inner pot which will also be known as a cooking pot.
- There will be an electric heating element, which acts as the heat source.
- There will be sensors that will electronically control the pressure and temperature.

The temperature and pressure sensor of the instant pot will ensure that an optimal environment is maintained all through the process.

Cooking with an instant pot is made even easier thanks to the plethora of various pre-programmed settings that comes with the pot.

The good number of these different buttons makes the process of cooking even more accessible.

The accuracy of these various pre-programmed settings is very high as the settings were chosen after assimilating the data from a huge number of chefs from around the world.

Understanding the buttons of Instant Pot

Due to the vast number of options available, individuals can become overwhelmed. Here is a brief overview of the functionalities of instant pot.

- **Sauté:** Utilize this button if you want to sauté your vegetables or other items in your inner pot while keeping the lid open. It is possible to adjust the level of brownness you desire by pressing the adjust button.
- **Keep Warm/Cancel:** Using this button, you can turn your pressure cooker off. Alternatively, you can use the adjust button to maintain a warm temperature.
- **Manual:** An all-rounder button which gives flexibility to the user. Using this button followed by the + or − you can set the exact cook time.
- **Soup:** This mode sets the cooker to high-pressure mode for 30 minutes (at normal); 40 minutes (at more); 20 minutes (at less).
- **Meat/Stew:** This mode sets the cooker to high-pressure mode giving 35 minutes cook time (at normal); 45 minutes (at more); 20 minutes (at less).
- **Bean/Chili:** This mode sets the cooker to high-pressure mode giving 30 minutes cook time (at normal); 40 minutes (at more); 25 minutes (at less).
- **Poultry:** This mode sets the cooker to high-pressure mode giving 15 minutes cook time (at normal); 30 minutes (at more); 5 minutes (at less).
- **Rice:** This is a fully automated mode which cooks rice on low pressure. It will adjust the timer all by itself depending on the amount of water/rice present inside the inner cooking pot.
- **Multi-Grain:** This mode sets the cooker to high-pressure mode giving 40 minutes cook time (at normal); 45 minutes (at more); 20 minutes (at less).
- **Porridge:** This mode sets the cooker to high-pressure mode giving 20 minutes cook time (at normal); 30 minutes (at more); 15 minutes (at less).
- **Steam:** This will set your pressure cooker to high pressure with 10 minutes cook time at normal, 15 minutes cook time at more and 3 minutes cook time at less. It is advised to use this mode with a steamer basket or rack for best results.
- **Slow Cooker:** This button will normally set the cooker at 4-hour mode. However, you change the temperature to 190-201F (at low); 194-205F (at normal); 199-210F (at high).

- **Pressure:** This button allows you to alter between high and low-pressure.
- **Yogurt:** This setting should be used for making yogurt in individual pots or jars.
- **Timer:** This button will allow you to decrease or increase the time by using the timer button and pressing the + or − buttons.

Crucial components of Instant Pot

By now you should have a good understanding of the fundamentals of the instant pot, now let me break down the different components of the instant pot.

Cooking Pot

The cooking pot is the place where the actual cooking takes place. These are mostly made from Stainless Steel or Aluminum.

High quality and premium electric pressure cookers such as the instant pot tend to go for stainless steel options that are easy to use and clean. Some models even opt for copper, which allows for even heat distribution.

Locking Mechanism

The sealing ring or gasket of the instant pot allows the device to create an air tight chamber inside the instant pot once the lid is closed.

When the upper lid is brought down and comes in contact with the inner pot, the gasket helps to create an internal vacuum that further helps to create delicious meals.

Safety Mechanism

As you may have already guessed, instant pots deal with a high amount of pressure and if this pressure is not maintained properly, things might get a bit drastic.

Thankfully though, the manufactures of electric pressure cookers and instant pots alike have mastered their craft and implemented very strong safety mechanism that make the instant pot extremely safe to use.

This mechanism comes in the form of 'push down pressure release' valves.

Newer electric programmable pressure cookers such as the Instant Pot tend to implement these valves, which come with their personal protection mechanism known as the 'anti block shield,' which protects them from any kind of wear or tear.

This technique allows the valves to stay intact as long as the specified pressure level has not been reached.

Once the pressure level exceeds normal levels though, the seal position of the valve slowly relaxes itself and allows any excess pressure to release in order to prevent excess buildup.

These new valves are also controlled by the accompanying electronic sensors; pressure and temperature that allow the cookers to hold a certain amount of pressure for a certain period of time.

Advantages of using Instant Pot
The core advantages of the Instant Pot include:

- **Save energy and time:** Thanks to the added pressure value of the instant pot, foods are cooked seventy percent faster in an instant pot when compared to other methods. This process uses less water while cooking and has a fully insulated exterior pot which minimizes energy loss, allowing even further lowering down of the energy required to boil, steam, or cook meals.
- **Preserve nutrients of the food while keeping things tasty:** Most traditional cooking methods require you to submerge your produces completely in water, which reduces the proteins and vitamins. With the instant pot, however, minimal liquid is used that prevents this from happening.
- **Kills harmful Micro-Organism:** Pressure cooker allows the internal temperature to reach high levels of heat where bacteria and viruses are killed off. Even the tough-to-kill ones.

Using Instant Pot

Using the Instant Pot is actually easy. The two things you need to know are:

"How the meals are cooked," and "How the pressure is released."

The process used in this book are known as 'water test.'

- Open up the lid of your Instant Pot.
- Add 1 or 2 cups of water to the inner pot of Instant Pot.
- Gently, move the valve to sealing position.

- Select pressure cooker timing; use the manual button to set it to 5 minutes.
- That's it. Now all you have to do is wait until the timer runs out. Within 5 minutes, the water should be heated up enough to have produced a good level of pressure.

Next comes the process of releasing the pressure:

There are actually two ways which the pressure can be released.

- **Quick Release:** This method is suitable for ingredients such as vegetables.
- **Natural Release:** This method is best suited for ingredients such as meat.

Cooking Guidelines

The following cooking times are meant as a guide. Through experimenting with your own instant pot you will have a better idea of the length of cooking time required. Please make sure the food is cooked before consuming. You can always return food to your instant pot to cook in 5 minute intervals until fully cooked.

Cook timetable: Fruits

Fruits	Fresh (minutes)	Dried/Frozen (minutes)
Apple – Slices	2 to 3	3 to 4
Apple – Whole	3 to 4	4 to 6
Apricot – Halves	2 to 3	3 to 4
Peach – Whole	2 to 3	4 to 5
Pear – Whole	3 to 4	4 to 6
Pear – Halves or Slices	2 to 3	4 to 5
Prune – Whole	2 to 3	4 to 5
Raisins – Whole	N/A	4 to 5

Cook timetable: Vegetables

Vegetable	Fresh (minutes)	Dried/Frozen (minutes)
Artichokes - Whole, trimmed	9 to 11	11 to 13
Artichokes – Hearts	4 to 5	5 to 6
Asparagus – Whole or Diced	1 to 2	2 to 3
Green or Yellow Beans – Whole	1 to 2	2 to 3
Beets – Whole, Small roots	11 to 13	13 to 15
Beets – Whole, Large roots	20 to 25	25 to 30
Broccoli – Florets	2 to 3	3 to 4
Brussel Sprouts – Whole	3 to 4	4 to 5

Cabbage; red, green, or purple – Shredded	2 to 3	3 to 4
Cabbage; red, green, or purple – Wedge	3 to 4	4 to 5
Carrots – Cut, Sliced	1 to 2	2 to 3
Carrots – Whole	2 to 3	3 to 4
Celery – Whole Stalk	2 to 3	3 to 4
Collards	4 to 5	5 to 6
Corn – Niblets	1 to 2	2 to 3
Corn on the Cob – Whole	3 to 4	4 to 5
Eggplant – Sliced	2 to 3	3 to 4
Endive – Whole	1 to 2	2 to 3
Escarole – Chopped	1 to 2	2 to 3
Green Beans – Whole	2 to 3	3 to 4
Leafy Greens	3 to 6	4 to 7
Leeks – Whole	2 to 4	3 to 5
Mixed Vegetables	2 to 3	3 to 4
Okra – Whole	2 to 3	3 to 4
Onions – Sliced	2 to 3	3 to 4
Parsnips – Sliced	1 to 2	2 to 3
Parsnips – Chunks	2 to 4	4 to 6
Peas in Pod	1 to 2	2 to 3
Peas	1 to 2	2 to 3

Potatoes – Cubed	7 to 9	9 to 11
Potatoes – Whole, Baby	10 to 12	12 to 14
Potatoes – Whole, Large	12 to 15	15 to 19
Pumpkin – Sliced	4 to 5	6 to 7
Pumpkin – Chunks	8 to 10	10 to 14
Rutabaga – Sliced	3 to 5	4 to 6
Rutabaga – Chunks	4 to 6	6 to 8
Spinach – Handful	1 to 2	3 to 4
Squash – Acorn, Chunks	6 to 7	8 to 9
Squash – Butternut, Chunks	8 to 10	10 to 12
Sweet Potatoes – Cubed	7 to 9	9 to 11
Sweet Potatoes – Whole, Small	10 to 12	12 to 14
Sweet Potatoes – Whole, Large	12 to 15	15 to 19
Sweet Peppers – Chunks or Sliced	1 to 3	2 to 4
Tomatoes – Quartered	2 to 3	4 to 5
Tomatoes – Whole	3 to 5	5 to 7
Turnips – Chunks	2 to 4	4 to 6
Yam – Cubed	7 to 9	9 to 11
Yam – Whole, Small	10 to 12	12 to 14
Yam – Whole, Large	12 to 15	15 to 19
Zucchini – Chunks or Slices	2 to 3	3 to 4

Cook timetable: Rice and Grains

Rice & Grain	Rice/Grain : Water	Cook (minutes)
Barley	1 : 4	25 to 30
Thick Textured Congee	1 : 4	15 to 20
Thin Texture Congee	1 : 6	15 to 20
General Couscous	1 : 2	5 to 8
Dried Corn (half)	1 : 3	25 to 30
Kamut portions	1 : 3	10 to 12
General Mill Oats	1 : 1⅔	10 to 12
Quick Cooking Oats	1 : 1⅔	6
Steel Cut Oats	1 : 1⅔	10
Thin Porridge	1 : 6	15 to 20
Quick Cooking Quinoa	1 : 2	8
Basmati Rice	1 : 1½	4 to 8
Brown Rice	1 : 1½	22 to 28
Jasmine Rice	1 : 1	4 to 10
White Rice	1 : 1½	8
Wild Rice	1 : 3	25 to 30
Sorghum	1 : 3	20 to 25
Cream of Wheat Berries	1 : 3	25 to 30

Cook timetable: Fish and Seafood

Seafood and Fish	Fresh (minutes)	Frozen (minutes)
Crab	3 to 4	5 to 6
Trout or Snapper – Whole	5 to 6	7 to 10
Fish Fillets – Whole (Cod, Haddock, Halibut)	2 to 3	3 to 4
Fish Steaks – Whole (Salmon, Tuna)	3 to 4	4 to 6
Lobster – Whole	3 to 4	4 to 6
Mussels	2 to 3	4 to 5
Fish/Seafood Soup/Broth	6 to 7	7 to 9
Shrimp or Prawn	1 to 2	2 to 3

Cook timetable: Beef, Chicken, Turkey

Meat	Fresh	Frozen
Stewing Beef	5 minutes per pound	10 minutes per pound
Beef Meatballs	5 minutes per pound	10 minutes per pound
Large Chunk: Chuck Blade, Rump, Steak, Brisket	5 minutes per pound	10 minutes per pound
Small Chunk: Chuck Blade, Rump, Steak, Brisket	5 minutes per pound	10 minutes per pound
Beef Ribs	5 minutes per pound	10 minutes per pound
Beef Shank	5 minutes per pound	10 minutes per pound

Beef Oxtail	5 minutes per pound	10 minutes per pound
Chicken Breast – Bone in	5 minutes per pound	10 minutes per pound
Chicken – Whole	5 minutes per pound	10 minutes per pound
Chickens Breast – Boneless	5 minutes per pound	10 minutes per pound
Chicken Drumsticks, Legs, or Thighs	5 minutes per pound	10 minutes per pound
Cornish Hen – Whole	5 minutes per pound	10 minutes per pound
Duck – Boneless, Pieces	5 minutes per pound	10 minutes per pound
Duck – Whole	5 minutes per pound	10 minutes per pound
Ham – Slices	5 minutes per pound	10 minutes per pound
Ham Shoulder – Whole	5 minutes per pound	10 minutes per pound
Lamb – Cubed	5 minutes per pound	10 minutes per pound
Lamb – Stewing	5 minutes per pound	10 minutes per pound
Leg of Lamb	5 minutes per pound	10 minutes per pound
Pheasant	5 minutes per pound	10 minutes per pound
Pork Loin Roast	5 minutes per pound	10 minutes per pound
Pork Butt Roast	5 minutes per pound	10 minutes per pound
Pork Ribs	5 minutes per pound	10 minutes per pound
Turkey Breast – Boneless	5 minutes per pound	10 minutes per pound
Turkey – Whole	5 minutes per pound	10 minutes per pound
Turkey Drumsticks	5 minutes per pound	10 minutes per pound
Veal Chops	5 minutes per pound	10 minutes per pound

| Veal Roast | 5 minutes per pound | 10 minutes per pound |
| Quail – Whole | 5 minutes per pound | 10 minutes per pound |

Cook timetable: Beans, Legumes, Lentils

Dried Beans & Legume	Dry (minutes)	Soaked (minutes)
Adzuki	20 to 25	10 to 15
Anasazi	20 to 25	10 to 15
Black Beans	20 to 25	10 to 15
Black-Eyed Peas	20 to 25	10 to 15
Chickpeas; Garbanzo, or Kabuli	35 to 40	20 to 25
Cannellini Beans	35 to 40	20 to 25
Glandules; Pigeon Peas	20 to 25	15 to 20
Unprocessed Beans	25 to 30	20 to 25
Green Lentils; French	15 to 20	20 to 25
Green Lentils; Mini	15 to 20	20 to 25
Red Lentils	15 to 18	20 to 25
Yellow Lentils	15 to 18	20 to 25
Lima Beans	20 to 25	10 to 15
Red Kidney Beans	25 to 30	20 to 25
White Kidney Beans	35 to 40	20 to 25
Navy Beans	25 to 30	20 to 25

Peas	15 to 20	10 to 15
Scarlet runners	20 to 25	10 to 15
Soy Beans	25 to 30	20 to 25

Instant Pot buying guide

Since there are multiple version of the Instant Pot out there in the market, the following should give you an idea of the one perfect for you.

The following 6 models are the more commonly used:

IP-DUO60

The most popular Instant Pot that boasts a 6 quart capacity, combines versatility of a pressure cooker, rice cooker, slow cooker, steamer, yogurt maker, Sauté/browning functionality in a single device.

There are 14 different functions and the device allows you to cook at HIGH or LOW pressures, which gives you further control over your meals.

At the time of writing it had a price tag of 99$ on Amazon.

IP-DUO Plus60

This is the updated model of the DUO60, now comes packed with additional features such as cake, egg, and sterilize settings. A unique alarm clock display provides a significant upgrade thanks to blue LCD display. The inner pot has also been updated. At the time of writing it had a price tag of 119.9$ on Amazon.

IP-DUO80

The DUO80 sports the same features as the DUO60 but larger capacity (8-quart) pot. At the time of writing it had a price tag of 129.99$ on Amazon.

IP-ULTRA

The ultra is the latest iteration of the Instant Pot and adds an ultra mode (along with normal settings) that allows you to further customize your cooking settings by controlling the temperature, pressure, and cook time. The features of the DUO-PLUS are included here as well. It also comes with an indicator that displays cooking progress. At the time of writing it had a price tag of 149.99$ on Amazon.

IP-Smart Bluetooth

The Instant Pot Bluetooth has all of the features of the IP-DUO but comes with the added feature of allowing you to control your device via Bluetooth.

At the time of writing it had a price tag of 159.99$ on Amazon.

IP-LUX60 V3

This device adds egg and cake setting to the pot, however, sacrifices the poultry, bean/chili, yogurt settings. Adds an option to cook at LOW Pressure.

It should be noted that it comes without some of the core accessories as well, so this is more of a budget option.

At the time of writing it had a price tag of 79.99$ on Amazon.

Chapter 3: Vegan And Vegetarian

Mashed Cauliflower

(Prep time: 5 minutes\ Cook time: 15 minutes\ 4 servings)

Ingredients

- 1½ cups of water
- 6 white potatoes, diced
- 1 cup cauliflower florets
- ½ tsp salt
- Pinch of fresh ground pepper
- 1 garlic clove, minced

Directions

1. Add water to the Instant Pot.
2. Add cauliflower and potatoes. Season with salt.
3. Lock the lid. Cook on HIGH pressure 5 minutes.
4. Release pressure naturally.
5. Season with pepper. Add minced garlic. Mash ingredients.
6. Enjoy!

Nutrition Value (Per Serving)

Calories: 229
Fat: 0.6g

Carbohydrates: 55g
Protein: 7.5g

Cauliflower Rice

(Prep time: 5 minutes\ Cook time: 10 minutes\ 4 servings)

Ingredients

- 1 cup of water
- 1 large cauliflower
- 2 Tbsp olive oil
- ¼ tsp salt
- ½ tsp dried parsley
- ¼ tsp cumin
- ¼ tsp turmeric
- ¼ tsp paprika
- Fresh cilantro
- Lime wedges

Directions

1. Wash the cauliflower and trim the leaves. Dice into florets.
2. Place steamer rack in instant pot. Transfer florets to the rack.
3. Pour in 1 cup of water.

4. Lock the lid. Cook on HIGH pressure for 10 minute.
5. Do a quick release. Drain off water.
6. Remove cauliflower.
7. Set pot to Sauté. Heat up the oil.
8. Return cauliflower to pot. Mash up with fork or masher.
9. Season with spices, and salt.
10. Stir. Squeeze in lime juice.
11. Serve. Garnish with cilantro.

Nutrition Value (Per Serving)

Calories: 169
Fat: 14g

Carbohydrates: 10g
Protein: 3g

Brussel Sprouts

(Prep time: 5 minutes\ Cook time: 5 minutes\ 4 servings)

Ingredients

- 2 pounds halved Brussel sprouts
- ¼ cup coconut aminos
- 2 Tbsp siracha sauce
- 1 Tbsp vinegar
- 2 Tbsp sesame oil (Allow Whole30 when used in small amounts)
- 1 Tbsp chopped almonds
- 1 tsp red pepper flakes
- 2 tsp garlic powder
- 1 tsp onion powder
- 1 Tbsp smoked paprika
- ½ Tbsp cayenne pepper
- Pinch of salt and pepper

Directions

1. Set instant pot to Sauté mode. Heat 1 teaspoon of sesame oil. Toast almonds 5 minutes. Take out. Let cool. Smash into smaller bits. Set aside.
2. To the instant pot, add coconut aminos, siracha, vinegar, sesame oil, red pepper flakes, garlic powder, onion powder, paprika, salt, pepper. Whisk to combine.
3. Add Brussel sprouts to pot. Stir to coat evenly.
4. Lock the lid. Cook on HIGH pressure 5 minutes.
5. Release pressure naturally.
6. Serve on a platter. Garnish with smashed almonds.

Nutrition Value (Per Serving)

Calories: 84
Fat: 7g

Carbohydrates: 5g
Protein: 2g

Baked Potato

(Prep time: 5 minutes\ Cook time: 20 minutes\ 4 servings)

Ingredients

- 1 cup of water
- 6 – 8 medium baking potatoes

Directions

1. Scrub the potatoes. Pierce with fork in a few places (lets out steam).
2. Place potatoes in instant pot.
3. Add water.
4. Lock the lid. Cook on HIGH pressure 10 minutes.
5. Preheat oven to 450F.
6. Allow pressure to release naturally over 10 minutes.
7. Using tongs, remove potatoes. Transfer to oven, middle rack. Bake 15 minutes.
8. Serve hot.

Nutrition Value (Per Serving)

Calories: 150
Fat: 0g

Carbohydrates: 39g
Protein: 6g

Squash Spaghetti and Garlic Sage

(Prep time: 5 minutes\ Cook time: 5 minutes\ 4 servings)

Ingredients

- 1 medium yellow squash
- 1 cup of water
- 2 Tbsp olive oil
- 1 small bunch fresh sage
- 3 garlic cloves, minced
- 1 tsp salt
- Pinch of nutmeg
- Fresh parsley

Directions

1. Halve the squash. Scoop out the seeds.
2. Add water to instant pot. Place trivet in pot.
3. Place the squash on the trivet, flesh side up.
4. Stack squash on top of each other.
5. Lock the lid. Cook on HIGH pressure 5 minutes.
6. In a medium pot, heat olive oil. Add sage, garlic, salt, nutmeg. Simmer 5 minutes.
7. Once cooking completed, release pressure naturally.
8. Remove the squash. Using a fork, strip the squash out.

9. Transfer spaghetti squash to the pot. Stir until coated.
10. Pour onto a serving platter. Garnish with parsley.

Nutrition Value (Per Serving)

Calories: 88
Fat: 4g
Carbohydrates: 13g
Protein: 1.5g

Garlic Mashed Potatoes

(Prep time: 5 minutes\ Cook time: 5 minutes\ 4 servings)

Ingredients

- 4 medium russet potatoes
- 1 cup vegetable broth
- 6 garlic cloves, minced
- ¼ - ½ cup almond milk
- Pinch of salt, pepper
- ¼ cup chopped parsley

Directions

1. Peel, rinse, then chop potatoes into chunks.
2. Transfer potatoes to instant pot.
3. Add broth and garlic.
4. Lock the lid. Cook on HIGH pressure 5 minutes.
5. Release pressure naturally.
6. Mash the potatoes using a masher.
7. Add almond milk. Stir. If they are too dry, add a bit more for desired consistency.
8. Serve in a bowl. Garnish with parsley.

Nutrition Value (Per Serving)

Calories: 293
Fat: 14g
Carbohydrates: 35g
Protein: 8g

Pickled Chilies

(Prep time: 10 minutes\ Cook time: 10 minutes \ 2 servings)

Ingredients

- 1 pound green chilies
- 1½ cup apple cider vinegar
- 1 tsp pickling salt
- 1½ tsp date paste

- ¼ tsp garlic powder

Directions

1. Add listed ingredients to instant pot.
2. Lock the lid. Cook on HIGH pressure 10 minutes.
3. Release pressure naturally.
4. Spoon mixture into sanitized jars, add 1 tablespoon of liquid.
5. Seal jars. Allow to set for twenty-four hours.

Nutrition Value (Per Serving)

Calories: 3.1
Fat: 0g

Carbohydrates: 0.6g
Protein: 0.1g

Zucchini Pasta Pesto

(Prep time: 3 minutes\ Cook time: 10 minutes \ 4 servings)

Ingredients

- 1 Tbsp olive oil
- 1 onion, chopped
- 3 large zucchini, sliced
- ½ cup of water
- 1½ tsp salt
- 1 bunch of basil leaves (picked off)
- 2 garlic cloves, minced
- 1 Tbsp extra virgin olive oil
- Extra zucchini for making Zoodles

Directions

1. Set instant pot to Sauté.
2. Heat olive oil. Sauté onion and garlic 5 minutes.
3. Add zucchini, water, and salt.
4. Lock the lid. Cook on HIGH pressure 5 minutes.
5. Release pressure naturally. Add basil.
6. Using an immersion blender, blend the ingredients to a pesto consistency.
7. Spin extra zucchini through Spiralizer to create zoodles.
8. Toss Zoodles with sauce. Serve. Garnish with fresh basil.

Nutrition Value (Per Serving)

Calories: 71
Fat: 4.7

Carbohydrates: 7.5g
Protein: 1.2g

Mexican Pinto Bean

(Prep time: 5 minutes\ Cook time: 30 minutes\ 4 servings)

Ingredients

- 1 pound dried pinto beans
- 1 tsp olive oil
- 1 small yellow onion, chopped
- ¼ red onion, chopped
- 3 garlic cloves, minced
- 2 scallions, chopped
- 1 can diced green Chilies
- 1 jalapeno, diced
- 2 bay leaves
- 1 tsp kosher salt
- 2 medium tomatoes, seeded, cored, chopped
- ¼ cup cilantro, minced
- ½ avocado, sliced
- Lime wedge for serving

Directions

1. Soak the pinto beans overnight. Discard the water.
2. Set instant pot to Sauté mode. Heat olive oil. Sauté yellow onion, red onion, garlic 5 minutes.
3. Add cilantro and cook 1 minute. Add pinto beans, jalapeno, tomatoes, green chilies, bay leaves. Pour in 6 cups of water. Stir well.
4. Cover the lid. Cook on HIGH pressure 30 minutes.
5. Release pressure naturally over 10 minutes. Remove bay leaves.
6. Serve in bowls. Garnish with avocado, lime wedge.

Nutrition Value (Per Serving)

Calories: 294
Fat: 8g

Carbohydrates: 42g
Protein: 17g

Stuffed Acorn Squash

(Prep time: 25 minutes\ Cook time: 30 minutes\ 2 servings)

Ingredients

- ¾ cup dry chickpeas
- ¼ cup brown rice
- 2 cups water
- 1 small acorn squash, halved, deseeded
- 1 tsp olive oil
- ½ tsp cumin seeds
- ½ small red onion, diced
- 4 garlic cloves, finely chopped
- Pinch of ground ginger
- Pinch of red pepper flakes
- ¼ tsp turmeric

- ½ tsp Garam masala
- ½ tsp lime juice
- 2 small tomatoes, chopped
- 1 cup spinach, chopped
- ½ tsp salt, fresh black pepper
- ¼ tsp cayenne pepper
- Garnish: Fresh cilantro

Directions

1. Soak chickpeas overnight. Soak brown rice 30 minutes prior to cooking.
2. Set instant pot to Sauté. Heat olive oil. Sauté cumin seeds 1 minute. Add onion, red pepper flakes, garlic, ginger, salt, pepper. Cook 5 minutes.
3. Add turmeric, garam masala, cayenne pepper. Stir well.
4. Stir in lime juice, tomatoes, spinach. Cook 5 minutes until tomatoes are soft.
5. Add chickpeas, rice, and water. Stir well.
6. Place a steamer rack over chickpea mixture. Place squash on steamer.
7. Lock the lid. Cook high pressure 20 minutes.
8. Let pressure release naturally.
9. Remove the steamer basket. Stir chickpea mixture.
10. Spoon mixture into shells of squash. Garnish with fresh cilantro.

Nutrition Value (Per Serving)

Calories: 155
Fat: 9g

Carbohydrates: 17g
Protein: 3g

Mashed Vegetable Platter

(Prep time: 5 minutes\ Cook time: 10 minutes\ 6 servings)

Ingredients

- 1 vegan stuffed roast
- 2 tsp extra virgin olive oil
- 4 garlic cloves, minced
- 1 yellow onion, diced
- 4 white potatoes, diced
- 2 large carrots, diced
- 1 tsp sea salt
- ¾ cup vegetable broth
- ¼ tsp fresh ground black pepper

Directions

1. Thaw vegan stuffed roast.
2. Set instant pot to Sauté. Heat the olive oil. Sauté onion, garlic 5 minutes.
3. Add potatoes, carrots, salt, and pepper. Stir.
4. Pour broth over vegetables. Place vegan stuffed roast on top.
5. Lock the lid. Cook on HIGH pressure 10 minutes.
6. Quick release the pressure.

7. Remove vegan load. Mash the vegetables. Add almond milk, black pepper. Stir.
8. Slice roast. Side with mashed vegetables.

Nutrition Value (Per Serving)

Calories: 330
Fat: 13g

Carbohydrates: 39g
Protein: 213g

Potato And Beans

(Prep time: 5 minutes\ Cook time: 12 minutes\ 3 servings)

Ingredients

- 1 Tbsp olive oil
- ½ tsp cumin seeds
- 4 garlic cloves, chopped
- 1 green chili, chopped
- 2 cups green beans, chopped
- 2 yellow potatoes, cubed
- 2 tsp coriander
- ¼ tsp turmeric
- ¼ tsp red chili powder
- 1½ tsp salt
- 1 tsp dry mango
- Fresh parsley

Directions

1. Set instant pot to Sauté. Heat olive oil. Sauté cumin seeds, garlic, green chili 5 minutes.
2. Once cumin splutters, add green beans and potatoes.
3. Add spices, except mango. Stir well.
4. Lock the lid. Cook on HIGH pressure 5 minutes.
5. Release pressure naturally.
6. Add mango powder. Stir and cook 2 minutes.
7. Serve in bowls. Garnish with fresh parsley.

Nutrition Value (Per Serving)

Calories: 213
Fat: 9g

Carbohydrates: 33g
Protein: 5g

Lentil and Millet

(Prep time: 10 minutes\ Cook time: 18 minutes\ 6 servings)

Ingredients

- 1 Tbsp olive oil
- 1 cup leeks, sliced
- ¼ cup oyster mushrooms, thinly sliced
- 2 garlic cloves, minced
- 1 cup millet, rinsed
- ½ cup french green lentils, rinsed
- 2¼ cups vegetable broth
- ½ cup bok Choy, thinly sliced
- 1 cup snow peas
- 1 cup asparagus, cut in 1 inch pieces
- ¼ cup fresh parsley, rosemary
- Drizzle lemon juice
- Pinch of salt, black pepper

Directions

1. Set instant pot to Sauté. Heat olive oil. Sauté leek, garlic, mushrooms 5 minutes.
2. Add lentils and millets. Cook 1 minute.
3. Add the broth.
4. Lock the lid. Cook at high pressure 10 minutes.
5. Release pressure naturally.
6. Add bok Choy, asparagus, and peas.
7. Lock the lid again. Let it sit 3 minutes.
8. Open the lid. Stir in parsley, cilantro. Add lemon juice. Stir well.
9. Serve.

Nutrition Value (Per Serving)

Calories: 369
Fat: 12g

Carbohydrates: 53g
Protein: 16g

Refried Beans

(Prep time: 10 minutes\ Cook time: 30 minutes\ 5 servings)

Ingredients

- 2 cups dried pinto beans
- 1 Tbsp olive oil
- 1 large onion, diced
- 2 cups vegetable broth
- 4 garlic cloves, diced
- 1 jalapeno, seeded
- 1 tsp salt
- 1 tsp paprika
- 1 tsp chili powder
- 1 tsp cumin
- ½ tsp black pepper
- ½ cup salsa
- Fresh cilantro

Directions

1. Set instant pot to Sauté. Heat the olive oil. Sauté the onion, garlic 5 minutes.
2. Add the pinto beans, jalapeno, salt, paprika, chili powder, cumin, black pepper, and salsa. Stir well.
3. Pour in vegetable broth. Stir well.
4. Lock the lid. Cook on HIGH pressure 25 minutes.
5. Release pressure naturally. Stir.
6. Mash with a masher.
7. Serve in bowls. Garnish with cilantro.

Nutrition Value (Per Serving)

Calories: 205

Fat: 12g

Carbohydrates: 14g

Protein: 14g

Eggplant Spread

(Prep time: 5 minutes\ Cook time: 5 minutes\ 6 servings)

Ingredients

- 4 Tbsp olive oil
- 2 pounds eggplant
- 3 - 4 garlic cloves, minced
- 1 tsp salt
- ½ cup of water
- Juice from 1 lemon
- 1 Tbsp tahini
- ¼ cup black olives, sliced
- Few sprigs fresh thyme
- 1 – 2 Tbsp extra virgin olive oil

Directions

1. Peel eggplant in alternating stripes of skin and no skin.
2. Slice the eggplant into chunks.
3. Set instant pot on Sauté. Heat the olive oil. Sauté the garlic 2 minutes.
4. Add the eggplant chunks, cook until caramelized.
5. Add water and salt.
6. Lock the lid. Cook on HIGH pressure 3 minutes.
7. Release pressure naturally.
8. Add Tahini, lemon juice.
9. Using an immersion blender, puree the mixture until a hummus consistency.
10. Pour in serving dish. Garnish with fresh thyme, dash of olive oil, black olives.

Nutrition Value (Per Serving)

Calories: 155

Fat: 11g

Carbohydrates: 16g

Protein: 2g

Indian Dal

(Prep time: 5 minutes\ Cook time: 15 minutes\ 3 servings)

Ingredients

- 2 cups red lentils
- 6 cups of water
- 1 red bell pepper, chopped
- 1 yellow onion, chopped
- 3 garlic cloves, minced
- Juice from ½ a lemon
- 1 tsp turmeric
- 1 tsp curry powder
- 1 tsp minced ginger
- ¼ tsp cayenne pepper

Directions

1. Add listed ingredients to instant pot.
2. Lock the lid. Cook on HIGH pressure 15 minutes.
3. Release pressure naturally.
4. Spoon dal over brown rice.

Nutrition Value (Per Serving)

Calories: 50
Fat: 4.4g

Carbohydrates: 3.1g
Protein: 0.7g

Artichokes

(Prep time: 5 minutes\ Cook time: 10 minutes\ 4 servings)

Ingredients

- 2 medium artichokes
- 1 lemon sliced in half
- 2 Tbsp vegan mayo
- 1 tsp Dijon mustard
- 1 pinch paprika
- 1 cup of water

Directions

1. Wash artichokes. Remove any damaged outer leaves.
2. Trim the spins, cut topped edge.
3. Wipe the cut edges with lemon.
4. Slice the stem, set aside.
5. Add water to instant pot.
6. Add trimmed parts to steamer basket.
7. Place steamer basket in instant pot. Spritz with lemon.
8. Lock the lid. Cook on HIGH pressure 10 minutes.
9. Release pressure naturally.

10. Place artichoke in serving platter. In a separate bowl, combine vegan mayo and paprika. Serve warm.

Nutrition Value (Per Serving)

Calories: 77
Fat: 5g

Carbohydrates: 0g
Protein: 2g

Vegan Pasta Sauce

(Prep time: 10 minutes\ Cook time: 15 minutes\ 3 servings)

Ingredients

- 1 Tbsp olive oil
- ½ yellow onion, diced
- 1 red pepper, diced
- 3 garlic cloves, minced
- ¼ cup fresh basil, chopped
- ½ can tomato paste
-
- ½ can tomato sauce
- 1 large can diced tomatoes
- 1 pound rotini noodles
- 1 cup of water or ½ cup tomato juice
- Garnish: Fresh basil, fresh ground black pepper

Directions

1. Set instant pot to Sauté. Heat olive oil. Sauté onion, garlic, red pepper 5 minutes.
2. Add the diced tomatoes, basil. Stir in tomato sauce, tomato paste, water or tomato juice. Stir well.
3. Lock the lid. Cook on HIGH pressure 10 minutes.
4. Cook the pasta in a separate pot.
5. Release pressure naturally.
6. Serve over pasta. Garnish with fresh basil, black pepper.

Nutrition Value (Per Serving)

Calories: 304
Fat: 14g

Carbohydrates: 40g
Protein: 0g

8 Vegetable Stir Fry

(Prep time: 10 minutes\ Cook time: 12 minutes\ 4 servings)

Ingredients

- ½ tsp fenugreek seed powder
- ½ tsp black pepper
- ½ tsp ground cumin, turmeric, coriander, mustard powder
- ½ tsp cinnamon
- ½ tsp cayenne pepper
- 1 Tbsp olive oil
- 3 garlic cloves, minced
- 3 cups mixed vegetables; cauliflower, broccoli, green beans, carrots, red pepper, zucchini, potatoes – dice the vegetables
- Pinch of salt
- 2 Tbsp of water
- ¼ cup green peas
- Garnish: fresh lemon, cilantro

Directions

1. In a bowl, combine fenugreek seed powder, black pepper, cumin, turmeric, coriander, mustard powder, cinnamon, cayenne pepper. Stir to combine.
2. Set instant pot to Sauté. Heat the olive oil. Sauté garlic 2 minutes.
3. Add cauliflower, broccoli, green beans, carrots, red pepper, zucchini, potatoes (not the peas). Stir in spice mixture. Pour in water. Stir.
4. Lock the lid. Cook on HIGH pressure 5 minutes.
5. Release pressure naturally. Add peas and salt. Stir.
6. Lock the lid. Cook on HIGH pressure another 5 minutes.
7. Release pressure naturally.
8. Serve warm.

Nutrition Value (Per Serving)

Calories: 326
Fat: 17g

Carbohydrates: 36g
Protein: 16g

Cabbage Rice

(Prep time: 120 minutes\ Cook time: 20 minutes\ 8 servings)

Ingredients

- 2 cups basmati rice
- 2 Tbsp olive oil
- ½ cup mustard seeds
- ½ cup unsalted peanuts
- ½ tsp turmeric
- 15 - 20 curry leaves
- 2 Tbsp grated ginger
- 4 green chilies, minced
- 2 cups of water
- 8 cups shredded cabbage

- 1 - 2 tsp salt
- 2 Tbsp lemon juice
- ½ cup chopped cilantro
- 3 Tbsp fresh coconut, shredded

Directions

1. Rinse rice under cold water, then soak in warm water 2 hours.
2. Drain. Set aside.
3. Set instant pot to Sauté. Heat the olive oil. Toast mustard seeds 2 minutes.
4. Add peanuts. Sauté 1 minute.
5. Add turmeric, ginger, curry leaves, green chili. Mix well.
6. Add grated cabbage, rice, salt. Add water.
7. Lock the lid. Cook on RICE using default settings.
8. Release pressure naturally.
9. Serve in bowls. Garnish with cilantro and coconut.

Nutrition Value (Per Serving)

Calories: 240
Fat: 9g
Carbohydrates: 32g
Protein: 7g

Black-Eyed Peas

(Prep time: 45 minutes\ Cook time: 35 minutes\ 4 servings)

Ingredients

- 1 cup black-eyed peas, soak in water 2 hours
- ½ tsp cumin seeds
- 1 onion, diced
- 2 tomatoes, diced
- 2 Tbsp tomato paste
- ½ inch fresh ginger, grated
- 4 garlic cloves, minced
- 1 green chili, minced
- 2 cups of water
- 1 tsp salt
- ½ tsp turmeric powder
- ½ tsp chili powder
- 1 tsp coriander
- Garnish: fresh cilantro

Directions

1. Soak peas 2 hours. Drain. Set aside.
2. In a blender, combine onion, garlic, green chili. Pulse into smooth.
3. Set instant pot to Sauté. Heat olive oil. Toast cumin seeds 2 minutes.
4. Add onion/garlic paste. Stir as it cooks 3 minutes.

5. Add diced tomatoes, tomato paste. Season with salt, turmeric powder, chili powder, coriander. Stir well.
6. Cook 5 minutes, until mixture thickens.
7. Add black-eyed peas, water to instant pot.
8. Lock the lid. Cook on BEAN/CHILI 30 minutes.
9. Release pressure naturally.
10. Pour in serving dish. Garnish with fresh cilantro.

Nutrition Value (Per Serving)

Calories: 132
Fat: 1g

Carbohydrates: 9g
Protein: 1g

Pindi Chole

(Prep time: 10 minutes\ Cook time: 46 minutes\ 4 servings)

Ingredients

- 1 cup dried chickpeas
- 2½ cups of water
- 1 cinnamon stick
- 2 cardamom pods, slightly cracked
- 2 cloves
- 2 bay leaves
- ¼ tsp Indian sulphur salt (Kala Namak)
- 1 plain black tea bag

Sauce

- 1 tsp organic safflower
- 8 garlic cloves, minced
- 1-inch piece ginger, grated
- 1 medium onion, diced
- 2 tsp Chana masala (or mix 1½ tsp Garam masala, 1 tsp coriander powder)
- ¼ tsp cayenne
- 1 tsp dry mango powder
- 2 Tbsp water
- Garnish: fresh sliced onion, lemon juice, pepper flakes

Directions

1. Soak chickpeas in water 4 hours prior to cooking.
2. Add cinnamon stick, cardamom pods, cloves, bay leaves, Indian sulphur salt, and tea bag. Pour in water.
3. Lock the lid. Cook on HIGH pressure 25 minutes.
4. Once done, release pressure naturally. Remove bay leaves.

5. In a blender, combine garlic, onion, ginger, water. Pulse until smooth.
6. In a saucepan, heat the olive oil. Add the puree. Cook 10 minutes.
7. Add cayenne pepper, dry mango powder. Simmer 1 minute.
8. Add cooked chickpeas to the spice mixture. Simmer 10 minutes.
9. Serve in a bowl. Garnish with chopped onion, lemon juice, pepper flakes.

Nutrition Value (Per Serving)

Calories: 640
Fat: 28g

Carbohydrates: 80g
Protein: 24g

Vegetable Gumbo

(Prep time: 10 minutes\ Cook time: 10 minutes\ 4 servings)

Ingredients

- 3 Tbsp olive oil
- 1 red bell pepper, chopped
- 1 cup kidney beans, soaked overnight
- 1 cup cremini mushroom, sliced
- 3 garlic cloves, finely chopped
- 2 Zucchini, sliced
- 2 Tbsp tamari sauce
- 2 cups vegetable broth
- 1 tsp black pepper
- Garnish: vegan cheddar cheese

Directions

1. Add listed ingredients to instant pot.
2. Lock the lid. Cook on HIGH pressure 10 minutes.
3. Release pressure naturally over 10 minutes.
4. Serve in a dish. Garnish with vegan cheese.

Nutrition Value (Per Serving)

Calories: 227
Fat: 11g

Carbohydrates: 28g
Protein: 6g

Eggplant Sambar

(Prep time: 10 minutes\ Cook time: 30 minutes\ 4 servings)

Ingredients

- 1 tsp safflower oil
- ½ tsp black mustard seeds
- 2 dried chilies
- 10 curry leaves, coarsely chopped

- 3 garlic cloves, chopped
- ½ red onion, chopped
- 1 Tbsp Sambar Powder
- (or mix 2 tsp coriander powder, pinch of cumin, cayenne and black pepper)
- 2 tomatoes, diced
- ½ tsp ground turmeric
- 1 - 2 cups chopped eggplant
- ½ cup green pepper, chopped
- 1 tsp tamarind paste/pulp
- Garnish: fresh cilantro, lemon wedges

Directions

1. Set instant pot to Sauté. Heat the olive oil. Toast the mustard seeds 1 minute.
2. Add red chilies, curry leaves. Cook 30 seconds.
3. Add onion, garlic. Cook 5 minutes.
4. Add Sambar powder. Cook 30 seconds.
5. Add tomatoes and turmeric. Stir well. Cook 5 minutes.
6. Add vegetables and mix
7. Add drained split peas, water, and tamarind. Stir well.
8. Lock the lid. Cook on HIGH pressure 15 minutes.
9. Release pressure naturally. Add tamarind pulp if using.
10. Pour into dish. Garnish with cilantro, lemon wedges.

Nutrition Value (Per Serving)

Calories: 524
Fat: 28g

Carbohydrates: 64g
Protein: 8g

Smokey Gouda Sauce

(Prep time: 5 minutes\ Cook time: 5 minutes\ 4 servings)

Ingredients

- 1 zucchini, chopped
- ½ cup daikon, chopped
- 1 small cauliflower, diced into chunks
- 2 garlic cloves, peeled, left whole
- 1½ cups of water
- ½ cup raw cashews
- ¾ tsp salt
- 1 Tbsp smoked paprika
- 2 Tbsp plum vinegar
- 1 tsp brown rice vinegar

Directions

1. Add listed ingredients to instant pot.
2. Lock the lid. Cook on HIGH pressure 5 minutes.
3. Release pressure naturally.
4. Allow to cool.

5. Blend using handheld/immersion blender 2 minutes to smooth consistency.
6. Serve over pasta.

Nutrition Value (Per Serving)

Calories: 379
Fat: 28g

Carbohydrates: 13g
Protein: 22g

Daal Makhani

(Prep time: 10 minutes\ Cook time: 35 minutes\ 4 servings)

Ingredients

- 1 cup split lentils
- 2 Tbsp avocado oil
- 1 Tbsp cumin seeds
- 1 large onion, chopped
- 1 bay leaf
- 3 garlic cloves, minced+ 1 garlic clove, minced
- 1 tsp Garam masala
- 1 tsp salt
- 1 tsp turmeric
- ½ tsp black pepper
- ½ tsp cayenne pepper
- 2 tomatoes, diced
- 2 cups of water
- 2 Tbsp coconut oil
- 2 Tbsp ghee
- Garnish: fresh cilantro

Directions

1. Soak lentils in cold water overnight. Drain. Set aside.
2. Set instant pot to Sauté. Heat the avocado oil. Toast the cumin seeds 1 minute.
3. Add onion, garlic. Saute 3 minutes. Add bay leaf, ginger, garam masala, salt, turmeric, black pepper, cayenne pepper. Stir.
4. Add tomatoes. Cook 2 minutes to soften.
5. Add lentils, water. Mix well.
6. Lock the lid. Cook on HIGH pressure 30 minutes.
7. Release pressure naturally over 10 minutes. Stir in ghee.
8. Serve in a dish. Garnish with fresh cilantro. Serve with Naan bread.

Nutrition Value (Per Serving)

Calories: 286
Fat: 8g

Carbohydrates: 41g
Protein: 14g

Spinach And Potatoes

(Prep time: 10 minutes\ Cook time: 25 minutes\ 2 servings)

Ingredients

- ⅓ cup uncooked brown lentils
- 1 tsp olive oil
- 4 garlic cloves, minced
- 1 inch ginger, grated
- 1 green chili, chopped
- 2 large tomatoes, chopped
- ½ tsp Garam Masala
- ¼ tsp cinnamon
- ¼ tsp cardamom
- ½ tsp turmeric
- 2 potatoes, cubed
- ¾ tsp salt
- 1 cup of water
- 1 cup spinach

Directions

1. Soak lentils 1 hour.
2. Set instant pot to Sauté. Heat olive oil. Sauté garlic, chili, ginger for 5 minutes.
3. Add tomatoes, ginger, green chili, garam masala, cinnamon, cardamom, turmeric, salt. Cook 5 minutes.
4. Add potatoes, water, drained lentils, salt, spinach to instant pot. Stir.
5. Lock the lid. Cook on HIGH pressure 15 minutes.
6. Release pressure naturally over 10 minutes.
7. Serve warm.

Nutrition Value (Per Serving)

Calories: 213

Fat: 11g

Carbohydrates: 21g

Protein: 9g

Lentil Bolognese

(Prep time: 5 minutes\ Cook time: 15 minutes\ 3 servings)

Ingredients

- 1 cup washed black lentils
- 1 can (28 oz) fire roasted diced tomatoes
- 1 tsp olive oil
- 1 yellow onion, diced
- 4 garlic cloves, minced
- 3 medium carrots, diced
- 1 small can tomato paste
- 4 cups of water
- 2 Tbsp dry Italian seasoning
- Pinch of red pepper flakes
- Pinch of salt and pepper

- Balsamic vinegar
- Zucchini Zoodles

Directions

1. Add listed ingredients to instant pot, except red pepper flakes.
2. Stir well to combine everything.
3. Lock the lid. Cook on HIGH pressure 15 minutes.
4. Release pressure naturally.
5. Open lid. Drizzle balsamic vinegar. Stir well.
6. Season with salt. Serve over Zucchini Zoodles.

Nutrition Value (Per Serving)

Calories: 69
Fat: 24g

Carbohydrates: 95g
Protein: 31g

Picatta Potatoes

(Prep time: 5 minutes\ Cook time: 10 minutes\ 4 servings)

Ingredients

- 2 cups of water
- 4 russet potatoes, sliced
- 2 Tbsp coconut oil
- 1 onion, julienned
- 1 red pepper, sliced
- ¼ cup vegetable broth
- 2 Tbsp fresh lemon juice
- ¼ cup parsley
- Pinch of salt and pepper

Directions

1. Add potatoes to instant pot. Pour in water.
2. Lock the lid. Cook on HIGH pressure 5 minutes.
3. Release pressure naturally. Drain potatoes with colander.
4. Set instant pot to Sauté. Heat the coconut oil. Return potatoes to pot.
5. Stir in lemon juice and broth. Sauté 5 minutes.
6. Serve in platter. Garnish with fresh parsley, salt, pepper.

Nutrition Value (Per Serving)

Calories: 442
Fat: 19g

Carbohydrates: 30g
Protein: 33g

Mushroom and Green Pea Curry

(Prep time: 15 minutes\ Cook time: 8 minutes\ 4 servings)

Ingredients

- 1 cup mushroom (your choice)
- 1 cup green peas
- 1 Tbsp olive oil
- 1 tsp cumin seeds
- 1 inch ginger, grated
- 4 garlic cloves, minced
- 1 green chili, diced
- 1 large onion, diced
- 2 large tomatoes, diced
- 2 tsp salt
- 2 Tbsp cashew cream
- Fresh cilantro
- ½ tsp turmeric powder
- 1 tsp coriander
- ½ tsp chili powder

Directions

1. If you have a spice grinder, you can use that. Or a mortar and pestle. Combine the ginger, garlic, green chili, onion. Grind together.
2. Set instant pot to Sauté. Heat the olive oil. Toast the cumin seeds 30 seconds.
3. Once the seeds sputter, add spice mix. Cook 5 minutes.
4. Blend tomatoes to a paste. Add to pot.
5. Season with salt, pepper, turmeric, coriander, chili powder. Add mushrooms and green peas.
6. Lock the lid. Cook on HIGH pressure 2 minutes.
7. Quick release the pressure. Stir in cashew cream.
8. Pour into serving dish. Garnish with fresh cilantro.

Nutrition Value (Per Serving)

Calories: 216
Fats: 6g

Carbs: 33g
Fiber: 1g

Gourd Curry

(Prep time: 10 minutes\ Cook time: 15 minutes\ 3 servings)

Ingredients

- 2 gourds cut in ½ inch pieces
- 1 Tbsp olive oil
- 1 tsp cumin seeds
- 4 garlic cloves, finely chopped
- 1 inch ginger, grated
- 1 green chili, diced
- 1 large onion, diced
- 2 large tomatoes, diced
- 1 tsp lemon juice
- Fresh cilantro

- 2 tsp coriander powder
- ¼ tsp turmeric powder
- ½ tsp garam masala
- 2 tsp salt

Directions

1. Set instant pot to Saute. Heat the olive oil. Sauté garlic, ginger, cumin, green chilies 5 minutes.
2. Add diced tomatoes, salt, and spices. Stir.
3. Lock the lid. Cook on HIGH pressure 10 minutes.
4. Naturally release pressure.
5. Pour in serving dish. Garnish with fresh cilantro.

Nutrition Value (Per Serving)

Calories: 461
Fats: 36g

Carbs: 29g
Fiber: 1g

Marinara Sauce

(Prep time: 10 minutes\ Cook time: 15 minutes\ 3 servings)

Ingredients

- 2 Tbsp olive oil
- 1 onion, diced
- 1 garlic clove, minced
- 1 carrot, diced
- 2 cans diced tomatoes
- 1½ tsp dried basil
- 1½ tsp dried oregano
- ¾ tsp sea salt
- Pinch of fresh ground black pepper
- Fresh parsley

Directions

1. Set instant pot to Saute. Heat the olive oil. Sauté onion and garlic 5 minutes.
2. Stir in tomatoes, oregano, and basil.
3. Lock the lid. Cook on HIGH pressure 10 minutes.
4. Release pressure naturally. Using an immersion blender, pulse until smooth.
5. Pour in serving dish. Garnish with fresh ground black pepper, parsley.

Nutrition Value (Per Serving)

Calories: 524
Fat: 7g

Carbohydrates: 92g
Protein: 23g

Garlic and Broccoli Mishmash

(Prep time: 3 minutes\ Cook time: 10 minutes\ 3 servings)

Ingredients

- 1 broccoli head, cut in florets
- ½ cup of water
- 6 garlic cloves, minced
- 1 Tbsp peanut oil
- 1 Tbsp white wine vinegar
- Pinch of sea salt

Directions

1. Place steamer rack in instant pot. Add florets to rack.
2. Add water.
3. Lock the lid. Cook on LOW 5 minutes.
4. Prepare ice bath for broccoli.
5. Quick release instant pot.
6. Transfer broccoli to ice bath.
7. Remove water from instant pot. Set to Saute.
8. Heat peanut oil. Sauté garlic 1 minute. Return broccoli to instant pot.
9. Stir in white wine vinegar. Season with salt. Stir 30 seconds.
10. Transfer to serving dish.

Nutrition Value (Per Serving)

Calories: 101
Fat: 8g

Carbohydrates: 6g
Protein: 6g

Parsnip And Potato Mash

(Prep time: 5 minutes\ Cook time: 10 minutes\ 6 servings)

Ingredients

- 3 pounds Yukon gold potatoes, peeled, diced
- 1 pound parsnips, peeled, diced
- 1 tsp salt, pepper
- 4 Tbsp cashew cream
- Sprigs of parsley, rosemary

Directions

1. Add water to instant pot. Place steamer basket in instant pot.
2. Place diced potatoes and parsnip in steamer basket.
3. Lock the lid. Cook on HIGH pressure 10 minutes.
4. Do quick release.
5. Remove basket. Pour out liquid. Return vegetables to instant pot.

6. Season with salt, pepper, rosemary. Mash the vegetables. Stir in cashew cream.
7. Pour in serving dish. Garnish with parsley.

Nutrition Value (Per Serving)

Calories: 257
Fat: 11g

Carbohydrates: 39g
Protein: 4g

Garlic Potatoes

(Prep time: 5 minutes\ Cook time: 5 minutes\ 4 servings)

Ingredients

- 4 medium russet yellow potatoes, diced
- 1 cup vegetable broth
- 6 garlic cloves, sliced in half
- ½ cup non-dairy milk (your choice)
- Pinch of salt, pepper
- ¼ cup chopped parsley

Directions

1. Add potatoes, broth, and garlic to instant pot.
2. Lock the lid. Cook on HIGH pressure 5 minutes.
3. Release pressure naturally.
4. Mash potatoes using masher. Season with salt, pepper. Stir in non-dairy milk.
5. Transfer to serving dish. Garnish with parsley.

Nutrition Value (Per Serving)

Calories: 293
Fat: 14g

Carbohydrates: 35g
Protein: 8g

Millet Pilaf

(Prep time: 10 minutes\ Cook time: 15 minutes\ 4 servings)

Ingredients

- 1 Tbsp olive oil
- 1 onion, diced
- 2 garlic cloves, minced
- 1 cinnamon stick
- 1 cup chopped carrots
- 1 cup millet
- 1¾ cups of water
- ½ cup vegetable broth

- Pinch of salt
- Italian parsley

Directions

1. Set instant pot to Sauté, Heat olive oil. Cook onion, garlic 3 minutes.
2. Add diced carrot, cinnamon stick. Sauté for 30 seconds.
3. Add millet. Stir well. Pour in water and broth
4. Add water and broth. Stir.
5. Lock the lid. Cook on HIGH pressure 10 minutes.
6. Release pressure naturally.
7. Discard cinnamon stick. Fluff with a fork.
8. Season with salt and pepper.
9. Transfer to serving dish. Garnish with italian parsley.

Nutrition Value (Per Serving)

Calories: 347

Fat: 7g

Carbohydrates: 62g

Protein: 9g

Spicy Cauliflower

(Prep time: 10 minutes\ Cook time: 5 minutes\ 4 servings)

Ingredients

- 1 large cauliflower
- 2 Tbsp extra virgin olive oil
- 2 tsp paprika
- 2 tsp ground cumin
- ¾ tsp kosher salt
- 1 cup fresh cilantro
- 1 lemon, quartered
- 1½ cups of water

Directions

1. Place steamer rack in instant pot. Pour in water.
2. Remove leaves, trim core of cauliflower.
3. In a small bowl, combine olive oil, cumin, paprika, salt. Drizzle over cauliflower.
4. Lock the lid. Cook on HIGH pressure 5 minutes.
5. Quick release pressure.
6. Transfer cauliflower to cutting board. Dice into florets. Serve.

Nutrition Value (Per Serving)

Calories: 138

Fat: 7g

Carbohydrates: 18g

Protein: 5g

Vegan Dumplings

(Prep time: 25 minutes\ Cook time: 10 minutes\ 6 servings)

Ingredients

- 1 Tbsp olive oil
- 1 cup white mushrooms, minced
- 1½ cups minced cabbage
- ½ cup shredded carrot
- 2 Tbsp soy sauce
- 1 Tbsp rice wine vinegar
- 1 tsp fresh ginger, grated
- 1 tsp sesame oil
- 12 round vegan dumpling wrappers
- 2 green onions, diced.
- Soy sauce for dipping

Directions

1. Set instant pot to Sauté. Heat the oil. Sauté mushrooms 3 minutes.
2. Add cabbage, soy sauce, carrot, rice vinegar. Cook until liquid evaporates.
3. Remove liner from instant pot. Set on stove. Mix in sesame oil and ginger. Set aside to cool slightly. Lightly coat steamer basket with oil.
4. Assemble dumplings. Place small bowl of water beside work station.
5. Take a wrapper, add 1 teaspoon filling. Rub water around edge of wrapper. Fold in half. Press closed. Repeat until mixture used.
6. Place dumplings in steamer basket. Place in instant pot.
7. Lock the lid. Cook at LOW pressure 7 minutes.
8. Release pressure naturally.
9. Serve on platter. Garnish with green onion. Soy sauce on side.

Nutrition Value (Per Serving)

Calories: 354
Fat: 17g

Carbohydrates: 42g
Protein: 8g

Vegan Shepherd's Pie

(Prep time: 5 minutes\ Cook time: 15 minutes\ 4 servings)

Ingredients

- 1 Tbsp olive oil
- 1 cup diced onion
- ½ cup diced carrot
- ⅓ cup diced celery
- ½ cup diced turnip
- 1 cup French green lentils
- 1 bay leaf
- ½ tsp fresh rosemary
- 1¾ cup vegetable broth
- 1 - 2 Tbsp vegan Worcestershire sauce

- 1 - 2 tsp tamari
- 1 cup diced/canned tomatoes
- 1 Tbsp tomato paste
- 1 portion garlic mashed potatoes (recipe in book)

Directions

1. Set instant pot to Sauté. Heat the olive oil. Cook onion, celery, carrot 3 minutes.
2. Add lentils, turnip, bay leaf, thyme, rosemary, tomatoes, and broth.
3. Lock the lid. Cook at HIGH pressure 10 minutes.
4. As it cooks, heat a skillet on the stove. Add the flour. Cook 1 – 2 minutes to bring out toasty smell. Stir in Worcestershire sauce until combined.
5. Release pressure naturally. Stir in the flour mixture.
6. Lock the lid again. Cook another 3 minutes. Preheat oven to broiler.
7. Quick release the pressure.
8. Discard the bay leaf. Transfer mixture evenly between ramekin dishes.
9. Top with garlic mashed potatoes. Place ramekins on baking tray.
10. Place under broiler until a golden crust on potatoes. Serve.

Nutrition Value (Per Serving)

Calories: 345
Fat: 9g

Carbohydrates: 60g
Protein: 7g

Chapter 4: Grains

Healthy Oatmeal

(Prep time: 5 minutes\ Cook time: 10 minutes\ 10 servings)

Ingredients

- 2 Tbsp maple syrup
- 1½ tsp coconut oil
- ¼ tsp salt
- ½ tsp ground cinnamon
- 1 cup old fashioned rolled oats
- 1 cup apples, chopped
- ½ cup dried cranberries
- ¼ cup walnuts, chopped
- ½ cup fat-free milk, such as almond
- 2 cups of water

Directions

1. Set instant pot to Sauté. Heat the coconut oil. Add the oats. Cook 3 minutes.
2. Add maple syrup, cinnamon, salt, walnuts, and cranberries. Add water. Stir.
3. Lock the lid. Cook on HIGH pressure 7 minutes.
4. Allow pressure to release naturally.
5. Stir in almond milk. Serve in bowls. Garnish with fresh fruit, maple syrup.

Nutrition Value (Per Serving)

Calories: 343
Fat: 13g

Carbohydrates: 46g
Protein: 14g

Cinnamon Oatmeal

(Prep time: 5 minutes\ Cook time: 3 minutes\ 4 servings)

Ingredients

- 1½ cups steel cut oats
- 2 tsp ground cinnamon
- 1 tsp allspice
- 4 ½ cups of water
- 1½ cups pumpkin puree
- 1 tsp vanilla extract

Topping

- ½ cup coconut sugar
- ¼ cup walnuts
- 1 Tbsp ground cinnamon

Directions

1. Add the oats, ground cinnamon, allspice to your instant pot. Whisk quickly. Pour in pumpkin puree, water, and vanilla extract. Stir well.
2. Lock the lid. Cook on HIGH pressure 3 minutes.
3. In a separate bowl, combine the coconut sugar, walnuts, ground cinnamon. Whisk briskly to combine. Set aside for topping oatmeal.
4. Once oats ready, allow pressure to release naturally.
5. Serve in bowls. Top with walnut mixture and milk.

Nutrition Value (Per Serving)

Calories: 91
Fat: 2g

Carbohydrates: 18g
Protein: 3g

Berry Oatmeal

(Prep time: 5 minutes\ Cook time: 6 minutes\ 1 serving)

Ingredients

- 1 cup quick oats
- 1⅔ cups of water
- 1 cup fresh berries
- 1 banana, diced
- ¼ cup almond milk
- diced almonds
- coconut flakes

Directions

1. Add water and oats to instant pot.
2. Lock the lid. Cook on HIGH pressure 6 minutes.
3. Release pressure naturally.
4. Serve in bowls.
5. Top with diced banana, berries, almonds, coconut flakes, almond milk.

Nutrition Value (Per Serving)

Calories: 263
Fat: 12g

Carbohydrates: 36g
Protein: 5g

Peach Oatmeal

(Prep time: 5 minutes\ Cook time: 3 minutes\ 4 servings)

Ingredients

- 2 cups rolled oats
- 4 cups of water
- 1 peach, diced
- 1 tsp vanilla extract
- 2 Tbsp flax meal
- Chopped almonds
- Almond milk
- Maple syrup

Directions

1. Add oats, flax meal, vanilla extract, diced peach, and water to instant pot.
2. Lock the lid. Cook on PORRIDGE 3 minutes.
3. Release pressure naturally.
4. Serve in bowls. Optional topping: chopped almonds, maple syrup, or milk.

Nutrition Value (Per Serving)

Calories: 307
Fat: 6g

Carbohydrates: 45g
Protein: 22g

Veggie Risotto

(Prep time: 10 minutes\ Cook time: 10 minutes\ 2 servings)

Ingredients

- 1 Tbsp olive oil
- ½ cup onion, minced
- 3 garlic cloves, minced
- 3 cups diced; squash, eggplant, zucchini
- 1½ cups risotto rice
- 3½ cups vegetable broth
- 1 tsp salt
- ½ tsp black pepper
- 1 tsp oregano
- ½ cup fresh parsley
- 1 medium tomato, diced

Directions

1. Set instant pot to Sauté. Heat olive oil. Cook onion, garlic 3 minutes.
2. Add squash, eggplant, zucchini. Cook 5 minutes.
3. Add rice. Stir in vegetable broth. Season with salt, pepper, and oregano.
4. Lock the lid. Cook at HIGH pressure 5 minutes.
5. Quick release the pressure.
6. Add tomatoes and parsley. Let stand 5 minutes.
7. Serve in bowls.

Nutrition Value (Per Serving)

Calories: 172
Fat: 7g

Carbohydrates: 20
Protein: 8g

Asian Styled Quinoa

(Prep time: 5 minutes\ Cook time: 2 minutes\ 2 servings)

Ingredients

- 2 cups quinoa
- 4 cups of water
- 2 Tbsp soy sauce
- 2 Tbsp rice vinegar
- 1 thumb grated ginger
- ½ cup frozen mixed vegetables

Directions

1. Thaw the frozen vegetables.
2. Add listed ingredients to instant pot; excluding vegetables.
3. Lock the lid. Cook on HIGH pressure 2 minutes.
4. Release the pressure naturally.
5. Add thawed vegetables. Stir. Let sit 2 minutes.
6. Serve in bowls.

Nutrition Value (Per Serving)

Calories: 249
Fat: 12g

Carbohydrates: 25g
Protein: 12g

Mushroom Risotto

(Prep time: 5 minutes\ Cook time: 8 minutes\ 2 servings)

Ingredients

- 1 small white onion, diced
- 3 garlic cloves, minced
- 1 Tbsp olive oil
- ¼ cup mushrooms, diced
- 1 tsp salt
- 1 tsp thyme
- ½ cup white wine vinegar
- 3 cups vegetable broth
- 1 cup arborio rice
- ¼ cup lemon juice
- 2 cups fresh spinach
- Pinch of fresh ground black pepper

Directions

1. Set instant pot to Saute. Heat the olive oil. Saufte onion and garlic 3 minutes.
2. Add rice, broth, thyme, wine vinegar, diced mushroom.
3. Lock the lid. Cook on HIGH pressure 5 minutes.
4. Release pressure quickly.
5. Stir in spinach, black pepper.
6. Serve in bowls.

Nutrition Value (Per Serving)

Calories: 312

Fat: 17g

Carbohydrates: 32g

Protein: 5g

Steel Cut Oats

(Prep time: 5 minutes\ Cook time: 10 minutes\ 4 servings)

Ingredients

- ½ cup Steel Cut Oats
- 2 cups of water
- 1 Tbsp oil
- Pinch of salt
- Garnish: granola, dried fruits, nuts

Directions

1. Add listed ingredients to instant pot.
2. Lock the lid. Cook on HIGH pressure 10 minutes.
3. Release pressure naturally.
4. Optional: Garnish granola, or dried fruits, or nuts

Nutrition Value (Per Serving)

Calories: 125   Fat: 3g   Carbohydrates: 20g   Protein: 7g

Biryani

(Prep time: 5 minutes\ Cook time: 25 minutes\ 4 servings)

Ingredients

- 1 Tbsp olive oil
- ¼ cup onion, diced
- 1 garlic clove, minced
- 1 tsp cumin seeds

- ½ tsp turmeric seeds
- ½ tsp turmeric powder
- ¼ tsp salt
- 1 cinnamon stick
- 1 cup brown rice
- 1½ cup of water
- ¼ cup raisins
- ¼ cup tightly chopped mint
- Chopped up raw cashew nuts for garnish

Directions

1. Soak the rice in cold water for 10 minutes. Drain. Rinse. Set aside.
2. Set instant pot to Saufte. Heat the olive oil. Cook cumin seeds, garlic, onion, turmeric, cinnamon stick, and salt 2 minutes.
3. Add strained rice, raisins, and water.
4. Lock the lid. Cook on MULTIGRAIN 25 minutes.
5. Quick release the pressure.
6. Fluff with a fork.
7. Transfer to serving dish. Top with diced cashews, fresh mint.

Nutrition Value (Per Serving)

Calories: 241
Fat: 2g

Carbohydrates: 49g
Protein: 6g

Butternut Squash Risotto

(Prep time: 10 minutes\ Cook time: 10 minutes\ 2 servings)

Ingredients

- 1 Tbsp olive oil
- ½ cup onion, diced
- 3 garlic cloves, minced
- 1 red bell pepper, diced
- 2 cups butternut squash, diced
- 1½ cups risotto rice
- 3½ cups vegetable broth
- ¼ cup white mushrooms, diced
- 1 tsp each salt, black pepper
- ½ tsp coriander
- ¼ tsp oregano
- 3 cups of mixed leafy greens; spinach, chard, kale
- 1 large handful fresh parsley

Directions

1. Set instant pot to Sauté. Heat the olive oil. Cook the butternut squash, onion, bell pepper, garlic 5 minutes.
2. Add risotto rice, vegetable broth, mushrooms, salt, pepper, oregano, and coriander. Stir well.
3. Lock the lid. Cook on HIGH pressure 5 minutes.

4. Release the pressure naturally.
5. Stir in parsley and greens. Allow to set 5 minutes.

Nutrition Value (Per Serving)

Calories: 488
Fat: 19g

Carbohydrates: 53g
Protein: 19g

Irish Oatmeal

(Prep time: 1 minute\ Cook time: 14 minutes\ 4 servings)

Ingredients

- 2 Tbsp coconut oil
- 1 cup steel cut oats
- 3 cups water
- ½ tsp salt
- ½ tsp ground cinnamon
- Garnish: cashew cream, brown sugar

Berry compote

- 1 cup strawberries, ¼ cup blackberries, ¼ cup blueberries
- 3 Tbsp granulated sugar
- 1 Tbsp of water

Directions

1. Set instant pot to Sauté. Heat the coconut oil. Add oats. Cook 5 minutes.
2. Add water, cinnamon, and salt. Stir 1 minute.
3. Lock the lid. Cook on HIGH pressure 13 minutes.
4. Prepare berry compote. In a small saucepan, combine strawberries, blueberries, blackberries, sugar, and water. Simmer 5 – 10 minutes until tender.
5. Release pressure naturally of instant pot. Stir well.
6. Serve in bowls. Option: top with cashew cream, brown sugar, or berry compote.

Nutrition Value (Per Serving)

Calories: 86
Fat: 1g

Carbohydrates: 17g
Protein: 3g

Melba and Peach Oatmeal

(Prep time: 5 minutes\ Cook time: 10 minutes\ 6 servings)

Ingredients

- 1½ cups steel cut oats
- 5 cups of water
- ½ cup pure maple syrup
- Pinch of salt
- 2 cups peaches, sliced
- 1 cup fresh raspberries, sliced
- ¼ cup chia seeds

Directions

1. Add oats, salt, water, syrup, and peaches to instant pot.
2. Lock the lid. Cook on HIGH pressure 10 minutes.
3. Release the pressure naturally.
4. Sprinkle in chia seeds, raspberries over oatmeal.
5. Close the lid. Let it rest 5 minutes.
6. Serve in bowls.

Nutrition Value (Per Serving)

Calories: 217
Fat: 14g
Carbohydrates: 23g
Protein: 5g

Porridge

(Prep time: 5 minutes\ Cook time: 6 minutes\ 2 servings)

Ingredients

- 1 cup porridge or steel cut oats
- 2 cups water (depending on desired consistency, can add more water)
- Garnish: maple syrup, crushed pecans, or walnuts, or almonds (your choice)

Directions

1. Add listed ingredients to instant pot. Stir.
2. Lock the lid. Cook on HIGH pressure 6 minutes.
3. Release the pressure naturally.
4. Serve in bowls. Garnish optional.

Nutrition Value (Per Serving)

Calories: 88   Fat: 0g   Carbohydrates: 19g   Protein: 2g

Millet Porridge

(Prep time: 5 minutes\ Cook time: 6 minutes \ 3 servings)

Ingredients

- 2 cups millet flakes
- 1 cup of water
- 2 cups cashew cream
- 1 Tbsp coconut oil
- 1 tsp vanilla extract
- 1 cup almond butter
- 1 tsp cinnamon
- Garnish: maple syrup, crushed walnuts

Directions

1. Add the listed ingredients to instant pot.
2. Lock the lid. Cook on HIGH pressure 6 minutes.
3. Release pressure over 10 minutes. Stir.
4. Serve in bowls. Garnish with maple syrup, walnuts.

Nutrition Value (Per Serving)

Calories: 88
Fat: 0g

Carbohydrates: 19g
Protein: 2g

Red Lentil Rice

(Prep time: 5 minutes\ Cook time: 12 minutes\ 4 servings)

Ingredients

- 4 Tbsp olive oil
- 1 medium red onion, thinly sliced up
- ¾ cup red lentils
- ½ cup basmati rice
- 1 tsp powdered cumin
- 1 tsp powdered coriander
- 1 tsp freshly grated ginger
- ½ tsp red cayenne pepper
- 1 tsp salt
- 2 cups cauliflower florets
- 1 medium yukon gold potato, peeled, cubed
- 4 cups of water
- ½ cup frozen green peas
- 1 Tbsp coconut oil
- 1½ tsp cumin seeds
- 2 dried red chilies
- ½ tsp crushed red pepper
- 2 Tbsp fresh lime juice
- 1 Tbsp chopped up cilantro

Directions

1. Rinse the basmati rice under cold water.
2. Set instant pot to Sauté. Heat the olive oil. Cook onion 5 minutes.

3. Add red lentils, rice, cumin, coriander, ginger, cayenne pepper, salt, turmeric, cauliflower, potatoe, and water. Stir well.
4. Lock the lid. Cook on HIGH pressure 5 minutes.
5. Release the pressure naturally. Add the peas. Close the lid. Let it rest 5 minutes.
6. In a separate pot, heat the 1 tablespoon of coconut oil. Toast the cumin seeds and crushed red pepper 2 minutes.
7. Serve the rice in a dish. Garnish with lemon juice, cilantro.

Nutrition Value (Per Serving)

Calories: 341
Fat: 10g

Carbohydrates: 53g
Protein: 11g

Confetti Basmati Rice

(Prep time: 5 minutes\ Cook time: 10 minutes\ 4 servings)

Ingredients

- 1 Tbsp olive oil
- 1 medium onion, diced
- 1 bell pepper, diced
- 1 carrot, shredded
- Water as needed
- 2 cups basmati rice
- ½ cup peas
- 1 tsp salt
- Fresh parsley

Directions

1. Rinse the basmati rice under cold water.
2. Set instant pot to Sauté. Heat the olive oil. Cook onion, red pepper 5 minutes.
3. Add rice, salt, water. Stir.
4. Lock the lid. Cook on HIGH pressure 5 minutes.
5. Release the pressure naturally. Add the shredded carrot and peas. Stir. Close the lid. Let it set 5 minutes.
6. Serve on a platter. Garnish with fresh parsley.

Nutrition Value (Per Serving)

Calories: 270
Fat: 6g

Carbohydrates: 46g
Protein: 6g

Jasmine Rice

(Prep time: 5 minutes\ Cook time: 4 minutes\ 4 servings)

Ingredients

- 3 cups jasmine rice
- 3 cups water
- Fresh mint

Directions

1. Rinse the rice in cold water.
2. Add the rice and fresh water to instant pot.
3. Lock the lid. Cook on HIGH pressure 4 minutes.
4. Release the pressure naturally. Fluff with a fork.
5. Serve in a platter. Garnish with fresh mint.

Nutrition Value (Per Serving)

Calories: 198   Fat: 3g   Carbohydrates: 38g   Protein: 1g

Coconut Rice

(Prep time: 10 minutes\ Cook time: 10 minutes\ 6 servings)

Ingredients

- 1 cup Basmati rice
- 1 tsp saffron
- 1 Tbsp warm almond milk
- 2 Tbsp coconut oil
- 15 whole cashews
- 2 green cardamom pods
- 6 cloves
- ½ tsp salt
- 1 cup fresh grated coconut
- ¾ cup sugar
- 2 Tbsp raisins
- 1 tsp cardamom powder

Directions

1. Rinse the basmati rice in cold water.
2. Soak saffron in almond milk. Set aside.
3. Set instant pot to Sauté. Heat 1 tablespoon of coconut oil. Toast cashews 1 minute. Remove from instant pot. Set aside.
4. Add rest of the oil. Toast cardamom pods and cloves 15 seconds.
5. Add the rice. Toast for 1 minute.
6. Add water, salt. Stir.
7. Lock the lid. Cook on HIGH pressure 6 minutes.

8. Release the pressure naturally.
9. Open the lid. Add coconut, raisins, cardamom powder. Stir well.
10. Set instant pot to Sauté. Cook 5 minutes.
11. Serve in a dish. Garnish with saffron and cashews.

Nutrition Value (Per Serving)

Calories: 369

Fat: 14g

Carbohydrates: 55g

Protein: 6g

Polenta Bites

(Prep time: 5 minutes\ Cook time: 5 minutes\ 4 servings)

Ingredients

- 4 cups vegetable broth
- 1 cup Coarse Polenta
- ½ tsp salt
- ¼ cup rosemary, thyme
- 1 - 2 tsp Cajun, taco, or Italian spices

Directions

1. Add the polenta, broth, salt with your choice of seasoning to the instant pot. Whisk to combine.
2. Lock the lid. Cook on PORRIDGE 5 minutes.
3. Release the pressure naturally.
4. Scoop out with a melon baller scoop, or pour out into a square dish, cut out small squares. Allow to set 30 minutes before serving.

Nutrition Value (Per Serving)

Calories: 383

Fat: 2.3g

Carbohydrates: 74g

Protein: 25g

Spicy Pickled Green Chili

(Prep time: 10 minutes\ Cook time: 5 minutes\ 2 servings)

Ingredients

- 1 pound green chilies
- 1½ cups apple cider vinegar

- 1 tsp pickling salt
- 1½ tsp sugar
- ¼ tsp garlic powder

Directions

1. Clean the chilies in cold water.
2. Poke 4-6 holes gently in the chilies, will help to absorb liquid.
3. Add listed ingredients to instant pot.
4. Lock the lid. Cook on HIGH pressure 5 minutes.
5. Release pressure naturally. Allow to cool down 10 minutes before placing in sanitized jars.
6. Place chilies in jars gently. Spoon liquid/brine over chilies. Seal jars. Wipe any excess liquid off jars.
7. Allow to cool down to room temperature for 24-hours.
8. Place in fridge for 3 – 7 days before consuming.

Nutrition Value (Per Serving)

Calories: 3.1
Fat: 0g

Carbohydrates: 0.6g
Protein: 0.1g

Curried Mushrooms

(Prep time: 3 minutes\ Cook time: 5 minutes\ 2 servings)

Ingredients

- 1 cup mushroom, sliced
- 6 garlic cloves, crushed
- ¼ cup red wine
- 1 Tbsp curry powder
- ½ cup low sodium vegetable broth
- 2 tsp low sodium soy sauce
- Pinch of black pepper
- 1 Tbsp browning sauce
- Fresh parsley

Directions

1. Add listed ingredients to instant pot.
2. Lock the lid. Cook on HIGH pressure 5 minutes.
3. Quick release pressure.
4. Serve in a platter. Garnish with fresh parsley.

Nutrition Value (Per Serving)

Calories: 486
Fat: 7g

Carbohydrates: 71g
Protein: 37g

Spicy Roasted Potatoes

(Prep time: 5 minutes\ Cook time: 10 minutes\ 4 servings)

Ingredients

- 1 pound fingerling potatoes, peeled cubed
- 2 Tbsp vegan butter
- Pinch of salt
- Pinch of fresh ground black pepper
- 1 Tbsp red pepper flakes
- Lemon juice
- ¼ cup Italian parsley

Directions

1. Set instant pot to Sauté. Melt 1 tablespoon of the vegan butter. Add the potatoes.
2. Lock the lid. Cook on HIGH pressure 10 minutes.
3. Release the pressure naturally.
4. In a large skillet, melt other tablespoon of vegan butter.
5. Add the potatoes. Season with red pepper flakes, salt, pepper. Flip the potatoes. Cook 2 minutes per side to crisp.
6. Serve in a platter. Squeeze lemon juice over the potatoes. Garnish with italian parsley.

Nutrition Value (Per Serving)

Calories: 14

Fat: 6g

Carbohydrates: 20g

Protein: 4g

Chapter 5: Soups and Stews

Onion Soup

(Prep time: 5 minutes\ Cook time: 15 minutes\ 6 servings)

Ingredients

- 2 Tbsp avocado oil
- 8 yellow onions, sliced
- 1 Tbsp balsamic vinegar
- 6 cups vegetable stock
- 1 tsp salt
- 2 bay leaves
- 2 sprigs of thyme

Directions

1. Set instant pot to Saute. Melt the avocado oil. Sauté the onions. Season with salt.
2. Add balsamic vinegar to deglaze the pot.
3. Add stock, and bay leaves. Stir.
4. Lock the lid. Cook on HIGH pressure 15 minutes.
5. Release the pressure naturally.
6. Remove bay leaves and thyme stems.
7. Transfer to a bowl. Serve with crusty bread.

Nutrition Value (Per Serving)

Calories: 219
Fat: 7g

Carbohydrates: 32g
Protein: 9g

Lentil Soup

(Prep time: 20 minutes\ Cook time: 15 minutes\ 8 servings)

Ingredients

- 2 cups brown or green lentils
- 8 cups vegetable broth
- 1½ pounds large red potatoes, cubed
- ½ cup mushrooms, halved
- 1 large onion, diced
- 2 large carrots, sliced
- 2 celery stalks, diced
- 2 bay leaves
- 2 tsp water
- 4 garlic cloves, minced
- 1 Tbsp low sodium soy sauce
- 2 tsp dried thyme leaves
- 1 tsp dried and crushed rosemary
- 1 tsp poultry seasoning
- ½ tsp sage
- Fresh ground pepper

Directions

1. Finely wash the lentils. Put them in instant pot. Add water and broth.
2. Set instant pot to Sauté. Allow lentils to simmer as you chop up the vegetables.
3. Add the vegetables and rest of ingredients to instant pot.
4. Lock the lid. Cook on HIGH pressure 15 minutes.
5. Release the pressure naturally. Remove bay leaves.
6. If potatoes are tender, then soup is ready. Otherwise, close the lid. Let it rest a few minutes. If the soup seems too thick, add some water.
7. Serve in bowls.

Nutrition Value (Per Serving)

Calories: 266

Fat: 0.5g

Carbohydrates: 49g

Protein: 16g

Butternut Squash Soup

(Prep time: 5 minutes\ Cook time: 30 minutes\ 4 servings)

Ingredients

- 1 tsp extra virgin olive oil
- 1 large onion, diced
- 2 garlic cloves, minced
- 1 Tbsp curry powder
- 3 pounds butternut squash, peeled, cubed
- 3 cups water
- ½ cup coconut milk
- Garnish: pumpkin seeds, dried cranberries

Directions

1. Set instant pot to Sauté. Heat the olive oil. Cook the onions, garlic, and curry powder 5 minutes.
2. Add butternut squash, salt, and water. Stir.
3. Lock the lid. Cook on HIGH pressure 30 minutes.
4. Release the pressure naturally.
5. Open the lid. Using an immersion blender, pulse the mixture to smooth consistency. Stir in coconut milk. Season with salt and pepper.
6. Serve in bowls. Garnish with pumpkin seeds, cranberries.

Nutrition Value (Per Serving)

Calories: 124

Fat: 6g

Carbohydrates: 18g

Protein: 2g

Cream of Carrot Soup

(Prep time: 15 minutes\ Cook time: 15 minutes\ 2 servings)

Ingredients

- 1 Tbsp olive oil
- 5 medium potatoes, peeled, cubed
- 8 carrots, peeled, chopped
- ½ yellow onion, diced
- 3 garlic cloves, minced
- 1 Tbsp curry powder
- 1 tsp cayenne pepper
- 4 cups water
- 2 cups vegetable broth
- Fresh kale

Directions

1. Set instant pot to Sauté. Heat the olive oil. Sauté onion, garlic, potatoes, and carrots 5 minutes.
2. Add vegetable broth, cayenne pepper, curry powder. Stir well.
3. Add kale and water. Simmer 2 minutes.
4. Lock the lid. Cook on HIGH pressure 8 minutes.
5. Release the pressure naturally.
6. Using an immersion blender, pulse until smooth consistency.
7. Serve in bowls.

Nutrition Value (Per Serving)

Calories: 155
Fat: 11g

Carbohydrates: 16g
Protein: 2g

Cream of Pumpkin Soup

(Prep time: 5 minutes\ Cook time: 15 minutes\ 4 servings)

Ingredients

- 1 onion, chopped
- 2 Tbsp coconut oil
- 3 Tbsp almond flour
- 2 Tbsp curry powder
- 4 cups low sodium vegetable broth
- 1 cup water
- 4 cups pumpkin puree
- 1½ cups fat-free half and half
- 2 Tbsp coconut aminos
- 1 tsp lemon juice
- Pinch cayenne pepper
- Pinch of salt and pepper

Directions

1. Set instant pot to Sauté. Melt the coconut oil. Sauté onion 5 minutes.

2. Stir in flour, almond flour, curry powder, cayenne pepper, salt, and pepper.
3. Whisk in pumpkin puree. Continue whisking as you pour in the broth, coconut aminos, and lemon juice.
4. Lock the lid. Cook HIGH pressure 3 minutes.
5. Quick release the pressure.
6. Using an immersion blender, pulse until smooth consistency.
7. Set instant pot to Sauté again. Stir in half and half. Simmer 5 minutes.
8. Serve in bowls.

Nutritional Value (Per Serving)

Calories: 41
Fat: 4g
Carbohydrates: 1g
Protein: 1g

Cream of Celery Soup

(Prep time: 10 minutes\ Cook time: 30 minutes\ 3 servings)

Ingredients

- 2 Tbsp coconut oil
- 1 large celery root, chopped
- 1 medium onion, diced
- 4 garlic cloves, minced
- 3 cups vegetable broth
- Pinch of white pepper
- ½ tsp thyme
- ½ tsp salt
- ¼ cup almond milk
- ½ tsp lemon juice

Directions

1. Set instant pot to Sauté. Heat the coconut oil. Sauté the celery, onion, and garlic 5 minutes.
2. Pour in the broth, lemon juice.
3. Lock the lid. Cook on HIGH pressure 5 minutes.
4. Release the pressure naturally. Allow to cool 10 minutes.
5. Pour into blender. Pulse until smooth consistency.
6. Transfer back to instant pot. Stir in almond milk. Season with salt, pepper, and thyme. Simmer 10 minutes.
7. Serve in bowls.

Nutrition Value (Per Serving)

Calories: 21
Fat: 13g
Carbohydrates: 20g
Protein: 6g

Apple and Broccoli Soup

(Prep time: 5 minutes\ Cook time: 15 minutes\ 4 servings)

Ingredients

- 2 Tbsp olive oil
- White part from 3 medium leeks
- 2 shallots, chopped
- 1 Tbsp curry powder
- Pinch of kosher salt
- 1 head of broccoli, chopped in florets
- 1 apple, peeled, diced
- 4 cups vegetable broth
- Pinch of fresh ground black pepper
- 1 cup full fat coconut milk

Directions

1. Set instant pot to Sauté. Heat the olive oil. Sauté leeks, shallots, broccoli, apple, 5 minutes. Season with salt, pepper, curry powder.
2. Pour in vegetable broth.
3. Lock the lid. Cook on HIGH pressure 5 minutes.
4. Release the pressure naturally.
5. Using an immersion blender, pulse until smooth consistency.
6. Set to Sauté again. Pour in coconut milk. Simmer 5 minutes.
7. Serve in bowls.

Nutrition Value (Per Serving)

Calories: 160
Fat: 8g

Carbohydrates: 5g
Protein: 3g

Black-Eyed Peas Hummus

(Prep time: 10 minutes\ Cook time: 10 minutes\ 6 servings)

Ingredients

- 1 Tbsp olive oil
- 1 cup dried black-eyed peas
- ½ onion, chopped
- 3 garlic cloves, minced
- ¼ cup pecans, chopped
- 1 - 2 Tbsp lemon juice
- 1 Tbsp hot sauce
- 1 tsp smoked paprika
- 1 tsp salt
- Fresh parsley

Directions

1. Rinse the black-eyed peas. Drain.
2. Set instant pot to Sauté. Heat the olive oil. Sauté onion, garlic 5 minutes.
3. Lock the lid. Cook on HIGH pressure 10 minutes.

4. Release the pressure naturally. Allow to cool 5 minutes.
5. Transfer ingredients to food processor.
6. Add the pecans to a food processor. Pulse the ingredients until smooth consistency. Pour into a bowl. Stir in lemon juice, salt.
7. Pour into serving dish. Garnish with parsley.

Nutrition Value (Per Serving)

Calories: 133
Fat: 3.7g

Carbohydrates: 19g
Protein: 7g

Cream of Potato and Celery Soup

(Prep time: 15 minutes\ Cook time: 20 minutes\ 4 servings)

Ingredients

- 1 Tbsp olive oil
- 2 large leeks
- 1 large onion, chopped
- 1 celery root bulb, diced
- 3 celery stalks, diced (save leaves for garnish)
- 4 potatoes, peeled, cubed
- 1 tsp thyme
- ½ tsp garlic powder
- 1 bay leaf
- 1 tsp salt
- 1 tsp pepper
- 1½ tsp lemon juice
- ¼ tsp cayenne pepper
- 6 cups vegetable broth
- ½ cup fat free half and half

Direction

1. Set instant pot to Sauté. Heat the olive oil. Sauté the leeks, onion, celery root, potatoes, diced celery stalks 5 minutes.
2. Stir in thyme, garlic powder, salt, pepper, cayenne pepper, bay leaf.
3. Pour in the broth. Stir.
4. Lock the lid. Cook at HIGH pressure 10 minutes.
5. Quick release the pressure.
6. Remove bay leaf. Stir in lemon juice.
7. Using an immersion blender, pulse until smooth consistency.
8. Set to Sauté. Stir in the cream. Simmer 5 minutes.
9. Serve in bowls. Garnish with celery leaves.

Nutritional Value (Per Serving)

Calories: 350
Fat: 2g

Carbohydrates: 33g
Protein: 7g

Spiced Quinoa

(Prep time: 10 minutes\ Cook time: 120 minutes \For 10 servings)

Ingredients

- 2 cups quinoa
- 5 cups water
- ¼ cup honey
- 1 Tbsp coconut oil
- 2 tsp ginger
- 1 tsp ground cardamom
- 1 tsp ground cinnamon
- ¼ tsp ground nutmeg
- 5 cloves (wrap in mesh, tie up)
- ¼ tsp salt
- 1 cup coconut milk
- 1 cup raspberries
- Maple syrup

Directions

1. Rinse quinoa under cold water.
2. Add quinoa, honey, coconut oil, ginger, cardamom, cinnamon, nutmeg, cloves, and salt to the instant pot. Stir well. Add the water.
3. Lock the lid. Cook on SLOW 2 hours.
4. Release pressure quickly. Open the lid. Remove mesh cloth with cloves. Stir in coconut milk and berries.
5. Serve in bowls. Drizzle maple syrup over top.

Nutrition Value (Per Serving)

Calories: 140
Fat: 4g

Carbohydrates: 24g
Protein: 5g

Mushroom and Barley Bowl

(Prep time: 10 minutes\ Cook time: 20 minutes\ 8 servings)

Ingredients

- 8 cups vegetable stock
- ¾ cup pearl barley
- 1 pound baby belle mushrooms, sliced
- 1 medium onion, diced
- 2 celery stalks, diced
- 2 carrots, diced
- 4 garlic cloves, minced
- 4 sprigs thyme
- 1 sprig sage
- 1 tsp salt
- ¼ tsp fresh ground pepper

- ¼ tsp garlic powder

Direction

1. Add listed ingredients to instant pot. Stir well.
2. Lock the lid. Cook on HIGH pressure 20 minutes.
3. Release the pressure naturally over 10 minutes.
4. Stir. Serve in bowls.

Nutritional Value (Per Serving)

Calories: 296
Fat: 5g

Carbohydrates: 50g
Protein: 9g

Potato and Chard

(Prep time: 5 minutes\ Cook time: 9 minutes\ 2 servings)

Ingredients

- 2 Tbsp olive oil
- 1 tsp cumin seed
- 1 medium onion, diced
- 1 jalapeno pepper, diced
- ½ tsp turmeric
- 1 Tbsp fresh ginger, grated
- 1 tsp salt
- 2 medium sweet potatoes, peeled, cubed
- 1 tsp ground coriander
- ¾ cup water
- 1 bunch Swiss chard
- 1 can unsweetened coconut milk
- ¼ cup fresh cilantro, finely chopped
- Lime wedges

Directions

1. Set instant pot to Sauté. Heat the olive oil. Toast the cumin seeds 1 minute.
2. Add jalapeno, turmeric, ginger, sweet potatoes, turmeric, coriander 4 minutes.
3. Stir in water and coconut milk. Add the Swiss chard.
4. Lock the lid. Cook on HIGH pressure 5 minutes.
5. Quick release the pressure. Stir.
6. Serve in bowls. Garnish with lime and cilantro.

Nutrition Value (Per Serving)

Calories: 398
Fat: 25g

Carbohydrates: 33g
Protein: 13g

Egg Bowl Soup

(Prep time: 5 minutes\ Cook time: 10 minutes\ 12 servings)

Ingredients

- 4 cups cabbage/Cole slaw mix
- 2 cups shredded carrots
- 1 can bean sprouts, drained, rinsed
- ½ cup vegetable broth
- 2 tsp sesame oil
- ¼ cup soy sauce
- ¼ cup Teriyaki sauce
- 2 garlic cloves, minced
- 1 tsp onion powder
- ½ tsp ground ginger
- Pinch of salt and pepper

Directions

1. In a medium bowl, combine sesame oil, teriyaki sauce, soy sauce, garlic, ginger, and onion powder. Whisk together.
2. Add broth to instant pot. Add cabbage, bean sprouts, and carrots.
3. Pour in mixed sauces. Stir well to combine.
4. Lock the lid. Cook at HIGH pressure 10 minutes.
5. Quick release the pressure. Stir.
6. Serve in bowls. Season with salt and pepper.

Nutrition Value (Per Serving)

Calories: 334

Fat: 14g

Carbohydrates: 40g

Protein: 16g

Pumpkin Curry Soup

(Prep time: 5 minutes\ Cook time: 15 minutes\ 4 servings)

Ingredients

- 1 onion, chopped
- 3 Tbsp almond flour
- 2 Tbsp curry powder
- 4 cups low sodium vegetable broth
- 1 cup water
- 4 cups pumpkin puree
- 1½ cups fat free half and half
- 2 Tbsp soy sauce
- 1 tsp lemon juice
- Pinch cayenne pepper
- Pinch salt, pepper
- Coconut oil
- Olive oil

Direction

1. Set instant pot to Sauté. Heat olive oil. Sauté onion 5 minutes.
2. Season with salt and pepper.
3. Stir in coconut oil. Add flour, curry powder. Stir until smooth.
4. Whisk in water and broth.
5. Stir in pumpkin puree, brown sugar, soy sauce.
6. Lock the lid. Cook at HIGH pressure 5 minutes.
7. Quick release pressure. Remove the lid.
8. Using an immersion blender, pulse until smooth consistency.
9. Set instant pot to Sauté. Stir in half and half. Simmer 5 minutes.
10. Turn off the heat. Stir in lemon juice. Serve in bowls.

Nutritional Value (Per Serving)

Calories: 41
Fat: 4g

Carbohydrates: 1g
Protein: 1g

Tomato Basil Soup

(Prep time: 5 minutes\ Cook time: 35 minutes\ 10 servings)

Ingredients

- 2 tsp olive oil
- 1 cup celery, diced
- 1 cup carrots, finely diced
- 1 cup onion, finely diced
- 2 Tbsp flour
- 3½ cups vegetable broth
- 1¾ cups low fat milk
- 1 can (28 oz) whole plum tomatoes with juice
- 1 sprig fresh thyme
- ¼ cup fresh basil, chopped
- 2 bay leaves
- Pinch of salt, pepper

Direction

1. Set instant pot to Sauté. Heat coconut oil. Sauté carrots, onion, celery 5 minutes.
2. Add flour. Stir 1 minute. Whisk in almond milk until flour mixture is smooth. Whisk in broth. Stir until combined. Add can of tomatoes.
3. Season with basil, bay leaves, thyme. Stir.
4. Lock the lid. Cook at HIGH pressure 30 minutes.
5. Release the pressure naturally. Remove bay leaves, thyme sprig.
6. Using an immersion blender, pulse until smooth consistency.
7. Set instant pot to Sauté. Stir in milk. Simmer 5 minutes.
8. Serve in bowls. Garnish with fresh basil.

Nutritional Value (Per Serving)

Calories: 195
Fat: 8g

Carbohydrates: 20g
Protein: 8g

Bean Chili

(Prep time: 30 minutes\ Cook time: 12 minutes\ 12 servings)

Ingredients

- 2 Tbsp vegetable oil
- 1 large onion, diced
- 5 garlic clove, minced
- 6 cups tomato juice
- 1 cup water
- 1 Tbsp + 1 tsp chili powder
- 1 tsp garlic powder
- ½ tsp cumin
- Pinch of salt, pepper
- 7 cups canned or soaked kidney beans
- 2 cans diced tomatoes
- Fresh green onions, sliced

Directions

1. Set instant pot to Sauté. Heat the vegetable oil. Sauté onion and garlic 5 minutes. Stir in the chili powder, garlic powder, cumin, salt, pepper.
2. Add kidney beans, tomato juice. Stir.
3. Lock the lid. Cook at SOUP pressure 7 minutes.
4. Release the pressure naturally.
5. Serve in bowls. Garnish with green onions.

Nutrition Value (Per Serving)

Calories: 194
Fat: 6g

Carbohydrates: 29g
Protein: 10g

Vegetable Lentil Soup

(Prep time: 10 minutes\ Cook time: 15 minutes\ 6 servings)

Ingredients

- 1 Tbsp olive oil
- 1 small onion, minced
- 1 garlic clove, minced
- 1 medium potato, peeled, cubed
- 1 small sweet potato, peeled, cubed
- 2 medium carrots, peeled, diced

- 1 cup lentil blend; yellow or red
- 1 tsp thyme
- 1 tsp marjoram
- ½ tsp smoked paprika
- ¼ tsp rosemary
- Pinch of salt, pepper
- 5 cups water
- 1 bay leaf
- Garnish: fresh parsley, sliced green onion

Directions

1. Set instant pot to Sauté. Heat the olive oil. Sauté the onion, garlic, potato, sweet potato, carrot 5 minutes.
2. Stir in the thyme, marjoram, smoke paprika, rosemary, salt, and pepper.
3. Pour in the water. Add the bay leaf. Stir well.
4. Lock the lid. Cook on HIGH pressure 10 minutes.
5. Once done, release pressure naturally.
6. Serve in bowls. Garnish with fresh parsley or sliced green onion.

Nutrition Value (Per Serving)

Calories: 247
Fat: 1g

Carbohydrates: 51g
Protein: 11g

White Onion And Carrot Soup

(Prep time: 5 minutes\ Cook time: 10 minutes\ 4 servings)

Ingredients

- 3 Tbsp olive oil
- 1 large white onion, diced
- 2 garlic cloves, minced
- 1 medium carrot, diced
- 6 cups vegetable broth
- Pinch of red pepper flakes
- 1 small can (28 oz) tomato puree
- 1 can diced tomatoes
- 1 cup fresh basil, minced
- Pinch of salt and pepper

Directions

1. Set instant pot to Sauté. Heat olive oil. Sauté onion, garlic, and carrot 5 minutes.
2. Stir in pepper flakes, basil, salt, pepper, and diced tomatoes. Slowly incorporate the tomato paste. Once it is combined, add the broth. Stir well.
3. Lock the lid. Cook on HIGH pressure 5 minutes.
4. Release pressure naturally. Let the soup stand for 10 minutes.
5. Serve in bowls. Garnish with fresh basil.

Nutrition Value (Per Serving)

Calories: 364
Fat: 37g

Carbohydrates: 7g
Protein: 2g

Smoky Split Pea Soup

(Prep time: 5 minutes\ Cook time: 20 minutes\ 2 servings)

Ingredients

- 1 Tbsp olive oil
- 5 cups water
- 1 small onion, diced
- 1 medium sweet potato, diced
- 1 cup split peas
- ½ cup dried navy beans
- 3 bay leaves
- ½ tsp liquid smoke
- Pinch of salt and pepper

Directions

1. Set instant pot to Sauté. Heat the olive oil. Sauté onion, sweet potato 5 minutes.
2. Add split peas, navy beans, water, bay leaves, liquid smoke, salt, pepper. Stir.
3. Lock the lid. Cook on HIGH pressure 20 minutes.
4. Release pressure naturally. Remove bay leaves.
5. Serve in bowls.

Nutrition Value (Per Serving)

Calories: 360
Fat: 12g

Carbohydrates: 49g
Protein: 16g

Bean Stew

(Prep time: 30 minutes\ Cook time: 35 minutes\ 3 servings)

Ingredients

- 1 pound dried navy beans, soak over night
- 1 Tbsp olive oil
- 1 large onion, chopped
- 4 garlic cloves, minced
- 1 large red pepper, diced
- 1 jalapeno, seeded, diced
- 1 large can fire-roasted diced tomatoes
- 4 tsp smoked paprika
- 2 tsp dried oregano
- 1 tsp dried basil
- 1 large squash, peeled, diced
- Pinch of salt and pepper
- 5 cups water
- 1 bunch kale, remove stem, chopped
- ½ cup fresh basil, chopped

Directions

1. Set instant pot to Sauté. Heat the olive oil. Sauté onion, garlic, red pepper, jalapeno 5 minutes.

2. Add water, beans. Stir.
3. Lock the lid. Cook on HIGH pressure 30 minutes.
4. Quick release the pressure. Open lid.
5. Add squash, tomatoes. Stir in smoke paprika, oregano, basil, salt, pepper.
6. Cook on HIGH pressure 10 minutes.
7. Release the pressure naturally. Open the lid.
8. Add the kale. Close the lid for 2 minutes.
9. Serve in bowls. Garnish with fresh basil.

Nutrition Value (Per Serving)

Calories: 383
Fat: 2.3g

Carbohydrates: 74g
Protein: 25g

Cauliflower And Sweet Potato Soup

(Prep time: 15 minutes\ Cook time: 20 minutes\ 8 servings)

Ingredients

- 1 Tbsp olive oil
- 1 large onion, chopped
- 3 garlic cloves, minced
- 1 small jalapeno, diced
- ½ tsp cumin seeds
- 1 Tbsp ginger paste
- Pinch of salt, pepper
- ¼ tsp cayenne pepper
- 1 Tbsp mild curry powder
- Pinch of cinnamon
- 1 pound sweet potatoes, peeled, cubed
- 1 large cauliflower, cut in florets
- ½ cup chickpeas, drained, rinsed
- 1 medium can diced tomatoes
- 4 cups vegetable broth
- 2 - 4 cups water (depending on desired consistency)
- 1 Tbsp natural peanut butter

Directions

1. Set instant pot to Sauté. Heat the olive oil. Sauté onion, jalapeno, sweet potatoes, garlic 5 minutes.
2. Stir in cumin seeds, ginger paste, salt, pepper, curry powder, cayenne pepper.
3. Pour in the tomatoes, cauliflower, chickpeas. Stir in the broth and water.
4. Lock the lid. Cook on HIGH pressure 20 minutes.
5. Release the pressure naturally. Open the lid.
6. Set to Sauté. Stir in natural peanut butter. Simmer to thicken.
7. Serve in bowls.

Nutrition Value (Per Serving)

Calories: 181
Fat: 1.9g

Carbohydrates: 35g
Protein: 7.4g

Bean Chili

(Prep time: 15 minutes\ Cook time: 35 minutes\ 2 servings)

Ingredients

- ⅔ cup dry black beans
- ⅔ cup dry navy beans
- ⅔ cup dry pinto beans
- ¼ cup dry red lentils
- 1 large can (28 oz) diced tomatoes
- 1 small can (8 oz) tomato paste
- 2 Tbsp chili powder
- 1 Tbsp ground cumin
- 3½ cups vegetable broth
- 1 Tbsp olive oil
- 1 yellow onion, diced
- 2 celery stalks, diced
- Pinch of salt and pepper
- Garnish: green onion, diced

Directions

1. Set instant pot to Sauté. Heat the olive oil. Sauté onion, garlic, celery 5 minutes.
2. Add the beans. Stir in the chili powder, cumin, salt, pepper.
3. Pour in the tomatoes. Stir in the tomato paste. Pour in the broth.
4. Lock the lid. Cook on HIGH 30 minutes.
5. Once done, release pressure naturally.
6. Serve in bowls. Garnish with diced green onion.

Nutrition Value (Per Serving)

Calories: 405
Fat: 4g
Carbohydrates: 69g
Protein: 27g

Leafy Greens Soup

(Prep time: 30 minutes\ Cook time: 30 minutes\ 4 servings)

Ingredients

- 1 Tbsp olive oil
- 1 onion, chopped
- 4 garlic cloves, minced
- 3 carrots, diced
- 1 sweet potato, cubed
- ½ a cup of split peas rinsed up and drained
- ½ cup white mushrooms, halved
- 2 pound chopped greens; kale, Swiss Chard, bok Choy
- 2 tsp oregano

- 1 tsp celery salt
- 1 tsp thyme
- ½ cup fresh basil, chopped
- 6 cups water
- 1 Tbsp cashew butter
- 1 Tbsp lemon juice
- Pinch of salt and pepper
- Garnish: fresh lemon slice, fresh ground black pepper

Directions

1. Set the instant pot to Sauté. Heat the olive oil. Sauté onion, garlic, carrots, sweet potato, split peas, mushrooms 5 minutes.
2. Add the kale, swiss chard, bok choy.
3. Stir in the oregano, celery salt, thyme, basil.
4. Pour in the water. Stir well.
5. Lock the lid. Cook on HIGH pressure 20 minutes.
6. Release the pressure naturally.
7. Using a hand blender, pulse the soup until smooth.
8. Stir in the cashew cream to thicken soup. Simmer 5 minutes.
9. Serve in bowls. Garnish with lemon slice, black ground pepper.

Nutrition Value (Per Serving)

Calories: 225
Fat: 9g

Carbohydrates: 22g
Protein: 14g

Coconut and Tomato Soup

(Prep time: 10 minutes\ Cook time: 15 minutes\ 4 servings)

Ingredients

- 1 Tbsp coconut oil
- 1 red onion, diced
- 1 garlic clove, minced
- 6 large tomatoes, diced
- 1 tsp minced ginger
- 1 tsp salt
- ½ tsp ground cayenne pepper
- ¼ cup fresh cilantro, chopped
- 1 tsp ground turmeric
- 1 can coconut milk
- 1 Tbsp honey
- Garnish: cilantro, fresh ground black pepper

Directions

1. Set instant pot to Sauté. Heat the coconut oil. Sauté onion, garlic 5 minutes.
2. Add the tomatoes. Season with ginger, salt, cayenne pepper, ground turmeric. Stir well.
3. Lock the lid. Cook on HIGH pressure 5 minutes.

4. Release the pressure naturally.
5. Using an immersion blender, pulse to smooth consistency.
6. Set to Sauté. Stir in coconut milk and honey. Simmer 5 minutes.
7. Serve in bowls. Garnish with fresh cilantro, fresh ground black pepper.

Nutrition Value (Per Serving)

Calories: 196
Fat: 17g

Carbohydrates: 12g
Protein: 3g

Vegetable Stock

(Prep time: 5 minutes\ Cook time: 25 minutes\ 10 servings)

Ingredients

- 1 Tbsp coconut oil or olive oil
- 2 small onions, chopped
- 4 garlic cloves, minced
- 2 celery stalks, diced
- 2 carrots, chopped
- 2 bay leaves
- 1 dried shiitake mushroom, diced
- 6 cremini mushrooms, sliced
- 1 tsp whole peppercorns, crushed
- 2 Tbsp light soy sauce
- 8 cups water
- ½ cup dried herbs, your choice

Directions

1. Set instant pot to Sauté. Heat the oil. Saute onion, garlic, celery, carrots, shiitake mushroom, cremini mushrooms 5 minutes.
2. Stir in crushed peppercorns, dried herbs.
3. Pour in soy sauce, water. Add the bay leaves.
4. Lock the lid. Cook on HIGH pressure 20 minutes.
5. Naturally release the pressure. Remove bay leaves.
6. Strain broth through fine mesh. Allow to cool. Store in fridge.

Nutrition Value (Per Serving)

Calories: 22
Fat: 4g

Carbohydrates: 119g
Protein: 23g

Curry Dal Makhani

(Prep time: 10 minutes\ Cook time: 35 minutes\ 4 servings)

Ingredients

- 1 cup split lentils
- 2 Tbsp avocado oil
- 1 Tbsp cumin seeds
- 1 large onion, chopped
- 1 bay leaf
- 3 garlic cloves, minced
- 1 tsp Garam masala
- 1 tsp salt
- 1 tsp turmeric
- ½ tsp black pepper
- ½ tsp cayenne pepper
- 2 tomatoes, diced
- 2 cups water
- 2 Tbsp coconut milk
- Fresh cilantro

Directions

1. Rinse lentils under cold water.
2. Set instant pot to Sauté. Heat the avocado oil. Toast the cumin seeds. Crush with a wooden spoon.
3. Sauté onion, garlic. Stir in ginger, garam masala, salt, turmeric, black pepper, cayenne pepper. Add the bay leaf.
4. Add tomatoes, lentils. Stir in water.
5. Lock the lid. Cook on HIGH pressure 30 minutes.
6. Release the pressure naturally.
7. Set to Sauté. Stir in coconut milk. Simmer 5 minutes.
8. Serve in bowls. Garnish with fresh cilantro.

Nutrition Value (Per Serving)

Calories: 281   Fat: 10g   Carbohydrates: 38g   Protein: 12g

Cream of Mushroom Soup

(Prep time: 5 minutes\ Cook time: 20 minutes\ 6 servings)

Ingredients

- ¾ cup coconut oil
- 1 yellow onion, diced
- 2 garlic cloves, minced
- 2 cups white mushroom, sliced
- 2 potatoes, peeled, cubed
- ¾ cup white wine vinegar
- 1 tsp dried thyme
- Pinch of salt and pepper
- 3 cups unsweetened soy milk
- 1 cup vegan béchamel sauce
- Garnish: fresh parsley, ground black pepper

Directions

1. Set instant pot to Sauté. Heat the coconut oil. Sauté onion, garlic 3 minutes.
2. Add mushrooms, potatoes. Stir in thyme, salt, pepper. Cook 4 minutes.
3. Add white wine vinegar. Stir.
4. Lock the lid. Cook on HIGH pressure 8 minutes.
5. Release pressure naturally.
6. Open the lid. Using an immersion blender, pulse the soup a few times. For a somewhat lumpy but smooth consistency.
7. Set instant pot to Sauté. Stir in béchamel sauce, soy milk. Simmer 5 minutes.
8. Serve in bowls. Season with fresh parsley and ground black pepper.

Nutrition Value (Per Serving)

Calories: 442   Fat: 19g   Carbohydrates: 30g   Protein: 33g

<u>Black Bean Soup</u>

(Prep time: 10 minutes\ Cook time: 20 minutes\ 6 servings)

Ingredients

- 1 pound dried black beans
- 2 Tbsp extra virgin olive oil
- 1 large red onion, chopped
- 1 large red pepper, diced
- 5 garlic cloves, minced
- 1 bay leaf
- 2 tsp dried oregano
- 1 tsp salt, black pepper
- 2 Tbsp vinegar
- ½ cup red wine vinegar
- 4 cups water
- Garnish: chopped vegetable mix - red pepper, tomato, avocado, scallions

Directions

1. Soak beans overnight. Drain before using.
2. Set instant pot to Sauté. Heat the oil. Sauté red onion, red pepper, garlic 5 minutes. Stir in oregano, salt, pepper.
3. Add pre-soaked beans, vinegar, red wine vinegar, water and bay leaf. Stir.
4. Lock the lid. Cook on BEAN/CHILLI pressure 15 minutes.
5. Release the pressure naturally. Remove bay leaf.
6. Using an immersion blender pulse soup to smooth consistency.
7. Serve in bowls. Garnish with chopped vegetable mix.

Nutrition Value (Per Serving)

Calories: 249   Fat: 0.6g   Carbohydrates: 55g   Protein: 7.5g

Beet Borscht

(Prep time: 10 minutes\ Cook time: 35 minutes\ 6 servings)

Ingredients

- 3 large beets, peeled, cubed
- 3 celery stalks, diced
- 2 large carrots, diced
- 2 garlic cloves, minced
- 1 medium onion, diced
- 3 cups shredded cabbage
- 6 cups vegetable broth
- 1 tsp salt, pepper
- 1 bay leaf
- ½ Tbsp thyme
- ¼ cup fresh dill, chopped

Directions

1. Place steamer rack in instant pot. Add beets to steamer. Pour in water.
2. Lock the lid. Cook on STEAM pressure 10 minutes.
3. Quick release pressure. Return beets to instant pot.
4. Add carrots, garlic, celery, onion, bay leaf, cabbage, thyme, stock, and salt.
5. Lock the lid. Cook on SOUP pressure 25 minutes.
6. Release pressure naturally.
7. Serve in bowls. Top with sour cream.

Nutrition Value (Per Serving)

Calories: 268
Fat: 9g

Carbohydrates: 43g
Protein: 8g

Fennel And Cauliflower Soup

(Prep time: 10 minutes\ Cook time: 15 minutes\ 6 servings)

Ingredients

- 1 Tbsp coconut oil
- 1 white onion, diced
- 3 garlic cloves, minced
- 1 extra-large fennel bulb
- 1 pound cauliflower florets
- 1 cup coconut milk
- 3 cups vegetable broth
- 2 tsp salt

Directions

1. Set instant pot to Sauté. Heat coconut oil. Sauté onion, garlic, fennel 5 minutes.
2. Add cauliflower. Pour in vegetable broth. Season with salt and pepper.
3. Lock the lid. Cook on HIGH pressure 5 minutes.
4. Once done, release pressure naturally.
5. Using an immersion blender, pulse until soup is smooth.
6. Set to Sauté. Stir in coconut milk. Simmer 5 minutes.
7. Serve in bowls. Garnish with parsley.

Nutrition Value (Per Serving)

Calories: 512
Fat: 11g

Carbohydrates: 94g
Protein: 26

Chapter 6: Drinks and Smoothies

Mango And Ginger Infused Water

(Prep time: 5 minutes\ Cook time: 5 minutes\ 4 servings)

Ingredients

- 1 cup fresh mango, chopped
- 2 inch piece ginger, peeled, cubed
- Water to cover ingredients

Directions

1. Place ingredients in mesh steamer basket.
2. Place basket in instant pot.
3. Add water to cover contents.
4. Lock the lid. Cook on HIGH pressure 5 minutes.
5. Once done, release pressure quickly.
6. Remove steamer basket. Discard cooked produce.
7. Allow flavored water to cool. Chill completely. Serve.

Nutrition Value (Per Serving)

Calories: 209

Fat: 1g

Carbohydrates: 51g

Protein: 2g

White Hot Chocolate

(Prep time: 5 minutes\ Cook time: 6 minutes\ 2 servings)

Ingredients

- 3 cups coconut milk
- ¼ cup cocoa powder/butter
- 2 - 2½ Tbsp honey
- 2 tsp vanilla extract
- Pinch of sea salt

Directions

1. Add milk, cocoa powder/butter, honey, vanilla extract and salt to instant pot.
2. Lock the lid. Cook on LOW pressure 6 minutes.
3. Release pressure quickly.
4. Using a hand blender, blend contents 25 seconds.
5. Serve hot.

Nutrition Value (Per Serving)

Calories: 331
Fat: 14g

Carbohydrates: 47g
Protein: 4g

Peach And Raspberry Lemonade

(Prep time: 5 minutes\ Cook time: 5 minutes\ 4 servings)

Ingredients

- 1 cup fresh peaches, chopped
- ½ cup fresh raspberries
- Zest and juice of 1 lemon
- Water to cover ingredients

Directions

1. Place ingredients in mesh basket for instant pot. Place in pot.
2. Add water to barely cover fruit.
3. Lock the lid. Cook on HIGH pressure 5 minutes.
4. Once done, release pressure quickly.
5. Remove steamer basket. Discard cooked produce.
6. Allow flavored water to cool. Chill completely before serving.

Nutrition Value (Per Serving)

Calories: 77
Fat: 0g

Carbohydrates: 19g
Protein: 0g

Hot Apple Cider

(Prep time: 5 minutes\ Cook time: 15 minutes\ 4 servings)

Ingredients

- 7 medium apples, cored, quarter
- 1 orange, peeled, cut into segments
- 1 lemon, peeled, cut into segments
- ½ cup fresh cranberries
- 2 cinnamon sticks
- ½ tsp whole cloves
- ½ star of anise
- ½ cup honey
- Water to cover ingredients

Directions

1. Add apples, lemon, orange and cranberries to instant pot.

2. Add cinnamon stick, star anise, and cloves.
3. Pour in water to cover ingredients.
4. Lock the lid. Cook on HIGH pressure 15 minutes.
5. Release pressure naturally.
6. Mash fruit with masher to release juices.
7. Strain the liquid. Chill completely before serving.

Nutrition Value (Per Serving)

Calories: 153
Fat: 9g

Carbohydrates: 14g
Protein: 4g

Blueberry Lime Juice

(Prep time: 5 minutes\ Cook time: 5 minutes\ 4 servings)

Ingredients

- 1 cup fresh blueberries
- Zest and juice of 1 lime
- Water to cover contents

Directions

1. Place ingredients in mesh steamer basket for instant pot. Place in pot.
2. Pour in water to cover contents.
3. Lock the lid. Cook on HIGH pressure 5 minutes.
4. Once done, release pressure quickly.
5. Remove steamer basket. Discard cooked produce.
6. Allow flavored water to cool. Chill completely before serving.

Nutrition Value (Per Serving)

Calories: 86
Fat: 0g

Carbohydrates: 22g
Protein: 0g

Sweet Cranberry Juice

(Prep time: 5 minutes\ Cook time: 8 minutes\ 4 servings)

Ingredients

- 4 cups fresh cranberries
- 1 cinnamon stick
- 1 gallon filtered water
- ½ cup honey
- Juice of 1 lemon

Directions

1. Add cranberries, ½ of water, cinnamon stick to instant pot.
2. Lock the lid. Cook on HIGH pressure 8 minutes.
3. Release pressure naturally.
4. Once cool, strain liquid. Add remaining water.
5. Stir in honey and lemon. Cool completely.
6. Chill before serving.

Nutrition Value (Per Serving)

Calories: 184

Fat: 0g

Carbohydrates: 49g

Protein: 1g

Hot Peppermint Vanilla Latte

(Prep time: 5 minutes\ Cook time: 5 minutes\ 4 servings)

Ingredients

- 4 cups almond milk
- 2 cups coffee
- 1 tsp vanilla
- ¼ cup honey
- 23 drops peppermint oil

Directions

1. Add listed ingredients to instant pot.
2. Lock the lid. Cook on HIGH pressure 5 minutes.
3. Once done, release pressure naturally.
4. Serve warm.

Nutrition Value (Per Serving)

Calories: 279   Fat: 3g   Carbohydrates: 61g   Protein: 3g

Berry Shrub

(Prep time: 10 minutes\ Cook time: 20 minutes\ 4 servings)

Ingredients

- 1 cup of dried elderberries
- 2 cups of apple cider vinegar
- 2 cups of water
- 2 cups of honey
- ½ a cup of chopped fresh oregano

Directions

1. Add listed ingredients to instant pot.
2. Lock the lid. Cook on HIGH pressure 20 minutes.
3. Once done, release pressure naturally.
4. Pour ingredients through a sieve into a jar.
5. Allow to cool down. Chill.

Nutrition Value (Per Serving)

Calories: 127   Fat: 0g   Carbohydrates: 6g   Protein: 0g

Cooked Iced Tea

(Prep time: 2 minutes\ Cook time: 4 minutes\ 4 servings)

Ingredients

- 4 regular teabags
- 6 cups water
- 2 Tbsp honey

Directions

1. Add ingredients to instant pot.
2. Lock the lid. Cook on HIGH pressure 4 minutes.
3. Once done, release pressure naturally.
4. Allow to cool completely. Serve over ice.

Nutrition Value (Per Serving)

Calories: 22
Fat: 0g

Carbohydrates: 6g
Protein: 0g

Hibiscus Tea

(Prep time: 5 minutes\ Cook time: 10 minutes\ 4 servings)

Ingredients

- 2 cup dried hibiscus petals
- 10 cups water
- 1 Tbsp honey
- 1 tsp fresh ginger, grated
- Rind from 1 pineapple

Directions

1. Rinse hibiscus leaves thoroughly with cold water.
2. Remove the dust.
3. Add water, honey, and ginger to instant pot. Stir.
4. Stir in hibiscus petals and pineapple rind.
5. Lock the lid. Cook on HIGH pressure 10 minutes.
6. Once done, release pressure naturally.
7. Remove pineapple rind. Pass liquid through fine mesh strainer.
8. Cool completely. Chill before serving.

Nutrition Value (Per Serving)

Calories: 114

Carbohydrates: 28g

Fat: 0g

Protein: 0g

Apple Cinnamon Water

(Prep time: 5 minutes\ Cook time: 5 minutes\ 4 servings)

Ingredients

- 1 whole apple, diced
- 5 cinnamon sticks
- Water to cover contents

Directions

1. Place ingredients in steamer basket. Place in pot.
2. Add water cover contents.
3. Lock the lid. Cook on HIGH pressure 5 minutes.
4. Once done, release pressure quickly.
5. Remove steamer basket. Discard cooked produce.
6. Allow flavored water to cool. Chill completely before serving.

Nutrition Value (Per Serving)

Calories: 194

Carbohydrates: 12g

Fat: 0g

Protein: 0g

Wassail

(Prep time: 5 minutes\ Cook time: 10 minutes\ 4 servings)

Ingredients

- 8 cups apple cider
- 4 cups orange juice
- 5 cinnamon sticks
- 10 cloves
- ½ tsp nutmeg
- Zest and juice of 2 lemons
- 1 inch peeled ginger
- 2 vanilla beans, split or 2 Tbsp pure vanilla extract

Directions

1. Pour cider and orange juice in instant pot.
2. Place cinnamon sticks, nutmeg piece, cloves, lemon zest, vanilla beans in steamer basket.
3. If you didn't use vanilla beans, pour in vanilla extract. Add lemon juice.
4. Lock the lid. Cook on HIGH pressure 10 minutes.
5. Once done, release pressure naturally.
6. Discard contents of steamer basket.
7. Serve hot from the pot.

Nutrition Value (Per Serving)

Calories: 221

Fat: 0g

Carbohydrates: 42g

Protein: 0g

Instant Horchata

(Prep time: 5 minutes\ Cook time: 5 minutes\ 4 servings)

Ingredients

- 32 ounces rice milk
- 6 Tbsp honey
- 1 cinnamon stick, broken into small chunks

Directions

1. Add listed ingredients to instant pot.
2. Lock the lid. Cook on HIGH pressure 5 minutes.
3. Once done, release pressure naturally over 10 minutes.
4. Cool completely. Chill before serving.

Nutrition Value (Per Serving)

Calories: 226
Fat: 1g
Carbohydrates: 53g
Protein: 2g

Jamaican Hibiscus Tea

(Prep time: 5 minutes\ Cook time: 5 minutes \For 4 servings)

Ingredients

- 1 cup dried hibiscus flowers
- 8 cups water
- 1 Tbsp honey
- ½ tsp ginger, minced
- Juice of 1 lime
- Ice as needed

Directions

1. Add hibiscus flowers, water, honey, and ginger to instant pot.
2. Lock the lid. Cook on HIGH pressure 5 minutes.
3. Once done, release pressure naturally.
4. Cool completely. Transfer to glass decanter. Stir in lime Juice. Pour over ice.

Nutrition Value (Per Serving)

Calories: 197
Fat: 0g
Carbohydrates: 18g
Protein: 0g

Ginger Ale

(Prep time: 5 minutes\ Cook time: 30 minutes\ 4 servings)

Ingredients

- 1 pound fresh ginger, unpeeled, diced
- Juice and rind of 2 lemons
- 1 Tbsp honey
- 1 quart carbonated water
- Lime wedges
- Ice for serving

Directions

1. Place ginger and lemon juice in food processor. Pulse to smooth consistency.
2. Transfer puree to instant pot. Stir in honey.
3. Add lemon peel to instant pot.
4. Lock the lid. Cook on HIGH pressure 30 minutes.
5. Once done, release pressure naturally. Strain and chill.
6. Serve over ice.

Nutrition Value (Per Serving)

Calories: 108
Fat: 0g

Carbohydrates: 28g
Protein: 0g

Blackberry Italian Drink

(Prep time: 5 minutes\ Cook time: 15 minutes\ 4 servings)

Ingredients

- 1 cup blackberries
- 2 Tbsp honey
- 1 bottle sparkling water
- 1 lemon, sliced

Directions

1. Add 1 cup (non-carbonated) water to instant pot.
2. Add blackberries to instant pot.
3. Lock the lid. Cook on HIGH pressure 10 minutes.
4. Once done, release pressure naturally.
5. Mash the berries in instant pot. Transfer to dish. Allow to cool.
6. As blackberries cook, in a separate small saucepan with heavy bottom. Add honey. Simmer 5 minutes. Cool down.
7. To make the drink. Spoon 1 teaspoon honey. Pour in fruit mixture. Add carbonated water. Stir.

Nutrition Value (Per Serving)

Calories: 249
Fat: 0.6g

Carbohydrates: 55g
Protein: 7.5g

Chapter 7: Sauces

Bone Broth

(Prep time: 5 minutes\ Cook time: 120 minutes\ 4 servings)

Ingredients

- Chicken bones
- Assorted vegetables; carrots, potatoes, onions, celery, turnip
- Splash of apple cider vinegar
- Filtered water
- Salt

Directions

1. Add ingredients to instant pot. Cover with water. Add salt.
2. Allow to sit 30 minutes.
3. Lock the lid. Cook on SOUP pressure 120 minutes.
4. Once done, release pressure naturally.
5. Strain the broth. Discard ingredients. Cool completely.
6. Pour broth into jars. Store in fridge.

Nutrition Value (Per Serving)

Calories: 30
Fat: 44g

Carbohydrates: 6g
Protein: 69g

Vegetable Broth

(Prep time: 10 minutes\ Cook time: 60 minutes\ 4 servings)

Ingredients

- 4 cups vegetable - diced; carrots, zucchini, red pepper, orange pepper, celery
- 10 cups water
- 1 small onion, diced
- ½ tsp turmeric
- 1 tsp salt
- ½ tsp cumin
- 1 tsp pepper
- ½ tsp garlic powder
- ½ tsp onion powder
- 1 tsp thyme
- 1 tsp oregano
- ½ tsp paprika

Directions

1. Add listed ingredients to instant pot.

2. Lock the lid. Cook on HIGH pressure 60 minutes.
3. Once done, release pressure naturally.
4. Strain the broth. Discard ingredients. Cool completely.
5. Pour into jars. Store in fridge.

Nutrition Value (Per Serving)

Calories: 20

Fat: 10g

Carbohydrates: 3g

Protein: 4g

Worcestershire Sauce

(Prep time: 5 minutes \ Cook time: 15 minutes \ 4 servings)

Ingredients

- ½ cup apple cider vinegar
- 2 Tbsp water
- 2 Tbsp coconut aminos
- ¼ tsp mustard seeds
- ¼ tsp onion powder
- ¼ tsp garlic powder
- ⅛ tsp cinnamon
- ⅛ tsp black pepper

Directions

1. Add listed ingredients to instant saucepan.
2. Lock the lid. Cook on SOUP 15 minutes.
3. Once done, release pressure naturally.
4. Cool completely. Transfer to glass jar. Store in fridge.

Nutrition Value (Per Serving)

Calories: 170

Fat: 1g

Carbohydrates: 1g

Protein: 6g

Red Hot Sauce

(Prep time: 25 minutes\ Cook time: 2 minutes\ 5 servings)

Ingredients

- 1 pound Fresno Peppers (Cayenne, or your choice)
- ¼ cup carrots, shredded
- 6 garlic cloves, smashed
- 1 roasted red pepper (jarred), chopped
- 1 cup white vinegar
- ¼ cup apple cider vinegar
- ½ cup water
- 1 Tbsp smoked salt or sea salt

Directions

1. (You will want to use protective eye wear and gloves for this recipe.)
2. Cut ends off peppers. Place all ingredients in instant pot.
3. Lock the lid. Cook on HIGH pressure 2 minutes.
4. Once done, release pressure naturally. (Don't inhale fumes.)
5. Using an immersion blender, pulse until smooth consistency.
6. Depending on desired consistency, strain mixture or don't strain mixture.
7. Place in glass jars. Store in fridge.

Nutrition Value (Per Serving)

Calories: 1
Fat: 0g
Carbohydrates: 0g
Protein: 0g

Chapter 8: Seafood

Tuna Zoodles

(Prep time: 5 minutes\ Cook time: 18 minutes\ 4 servings)

Ingredients

- 1 Tbsp olive oil
- ½ cup red onion, diced
- 2 cups zucchini zoodles (1/2 cup per person, make more if you want more)
- 1 can italian spices diced tomatoes
- 1¼ cup water
- Pinch of salt, pepper
- 1 small can tuna in water
- 1 jar marinated artichoke hearts
- Garnish: fresh parsley

Directions

1. Set instant pot to Sauté. Heat the oil. Sauté onion 3 minutes. Add the tomatoes.
2. Add the zoodles, water. Stir.
3. Lock the lid. Cook on HIGH pressure 10 minutes.
4. Release pressure naturally over 10 minutes. Open lid.
5. Stir in artichokes, tuna.
6. Set instant pot to Sauté. Simmer 5 minutes.
7. Serve in bowls. Season with salt and pepper. Garnish with fresh parsley.

Nutritional Value (Per Serving)

Calories: 321   Fat: 17g   Carbohydrates: 51g   Protein: 53g

Salmon And Vegetables

(Prep time: 5 minutes\ Cook time: 10 minutes\ 6 servings)

Ingredients

- 2 medium salmon fillets
- 1 garlic clove, diced
- 1 small red chili, diced
- Pinch of salt and pepper
- 1 tsp date paste
- 2 Tbsp coconut aminos
- 1 cup mixed vegetables; carrot, zucchini, green beans, water chestnut
- 1 garlic clove, diced
- Juice ½ a lime
- 1 Tbsp tamari sauce
- 1 Tbsp olive oil
- ½ tsp sesame oil

Directions

1. Add 1 cup water to instant pot. Place steamer rack in pot.
2. Place salmon fillets in a heat-proof bowl. Season with pepper, garlic, chili.
3. In a small bowl, combine date paste, tamari sauce. Pour over salmon fillets.
4. Set salmon bowl in steamer rack,
5. Lock the lid. Cook on HIGH pressure 10 minutes.
6. Slice vegetables. Place in a steam basket.
7. Once the timer runs out, release the pressure quickly
8. Place steam basket with vegetables on top of salmon bowl.
9. Drizzle vegetables with lime juice, sesame oil, salt, and pepper.
10. Lock the lid. Set timer to 0 and HIGH pressure. Wait 1 minute.
11. Once done, release pressure quickly.
12. Remove steamer basket with vegetables. Transfer to plate.
13. Remove bowl with salmon. Transfer to plate on top of vegetables.
14. Pour any juices from instant pot over salmon and vegetables. Garnish with fresh dill, fresh ground pepper.

Nutrition Value

Calories: 236   Fat: 15g   Carbohydrates: 0g   Protein: 23g

Chili Salmon

(Prep time: 5 minutes\ Cook time: 5 minutes\ 6 servings)

Ingredients

- 1 pound salmon fillet, cut in 4 pieces
- Pinch of salt and pepper
- 1 Tbsp chili powder
- 1 tsp ground cumin
- 1 tsp garlic powder
- Juice from 1 lime
- Garnish: lime juice, avocado, fresh cilantro

Directions

1. Add water to instant pot. Place steamer rack in pot.
2. In a small bowl, combine ground cumin, chili powder, garlic powder. Whisk together.
3. Sprinkle lime juice over fillets. Season with spice rub. Transfer fillets to rack.
4. Lock the lid. Cook on HIGH pressure 5 minutes.
5. Once done, release pressure naturally release.
6. Serve on plate. Garnish with lime juice, lime slice, sliced avocado, fresh cilantro.

Nutritional Value (Per Serving)

Calories: 416   Fat: 23g   Carbohydrates: 22g   Protein: 30g

Orange and Salmon

(Prep time: 10 minutes\ Cook time: 15 minutes\ 4 servings)

Ingredients

- 4 pieces of salmon fillets
- 1 cup of orange juice
- 2 Tbsp of cornstarch juice
- 1 tsp of grated orange peel
- 1 tsp of black pepper
- Garnish: lemon slices, fresh parsley

Directions

1. Add listed ingredients to instant pot.
2. Lock the lid. Cook on HIGH pressure 15 minutes.
3. Once done, release the pressure naturally.
4. Serve on a plate. Garnish with lemon slices, fresh parsley.

Nutrition Value (Per Serving)

Calories: 583   Fat: 20g   Carbohydrates: 71g   Protein: 33g

Swordfish

(Prep time: 10 minutes\ Cook time: 10 minutes\ 6 servings)

Ingredients

- 5 sword fish fillets
- ½ cup melted clarified butter
- 6 garlic cloves, minced
- 1 Tbsp black pepper
- Garnish: lemon wedges, fresh dill

Directions

1. In a small bowl, combine the garlic, black pepper, clarified butter. Whisk.
2. Place 1 fillet on parchment paper.
3. Cover with seasoned butter. Wrap parchment around fillet. Repeat for all fillets.
4. Place in instant pot.
5. Lock the lid. Cook on HIGH pressure 10 minutes.
6. Once done, release pressure naturally.
7. Serve on a plate. Garnish with lemon wedges, fresh dill.

Nutrition Value (Per Serving)

Calories: 379
Fat: 26g
Carbohydrates: 1g
Protein: 34g

Fried Salmon Patties

(Prep time: 10 minutes\ Cook time: 16 minutes\ 2 servings)

Ingredients

- 2 salmon fillets
- ¼ cup onion, diced
- 2 celery stalks, minced
- 1 egg
- Almond meal as needed
- Pinch of salt and pepper
- 2 Tbsp olive oil
- 1 cup water

Directions

1. Add water to instant pot. Place steamer rack in pot.
2. Season fish with salt and pepper. Place in instant pot.
3. Lock the lid. Cook on HIGH pressure 10 minutes.
4. Once done, quick release the pressure.
5. Remove the fish and allow it to cool.
6. Break the fillets in a bowl. Add egg, yellow, and green onions. Mash together.
7. Add a couple tablespoons almond meal. Mix together.
8. Divide mixture into patties.
9. In a large skillet, heat the olive oil.
10. Cook the patties 3 minutes per side. Serve immediately.

Nutrition Value (Per Serving)

Calories: 238　　　　　　　　　　　Carbohydrates: 1g
Fat: 15g　　　　　　　　　　　　　Protein: 23g

Curry Tilapia

(Prep time: 10 minutes\ Cook time: 15 minutes\ 4 servings)

Ingredients

- 1 pound tilapia fillets, cut in 2-inch pieces
- 1 Tbsp olive oil
- ½ onion, diced
- ½ green pepper, sliced
- ½ yellow pepper, sliced
- 1 Tbsp ginger paste
- ½ tsp mustard seed
- 1 can coconut milk
- 10 curry leaves
- 1 tsp salt
- ½ tsp turmeric powder
- ½ tsp chili powder
- 2 tsp coriander powder
- 1 tsp cumin powder
- ½ tsp Garam Masala
- Fresh cilantro

- Fresh mint leaves
- ½ tsp lime juice

Directions

1. Set instant pot to Sauté. Heat the olive oil. Sauté the onion, garlic, green pepper, yellow pepper, and mustard seeds 5 minutes. Stir in garlic paste.
2. Add the turmeric, chili powder, coriander, cumin, garam masala. Stir well.
3. Whisk in the coconut milk. Simmer the ingredients for 1 minute.
4. Add the tilapia and curry leaves.
5. Lock the lid. Cook on HIGH pressure 10 minutes.
6. Once done, release the pressure quickly.
7. Serve on plates. Garnish with fresh cilantro, fresh mint, lime juice, lime wedges.

Nutrition Value (Per Serving)

Calories: 392

Fat: 27g

Carbohydrates: 12g

Protein: 29g

Coconut Curry Fish

(Prep time: 5 minutes\ Cook time: 5 minutes\ 4 servings)

Ingredients

- 1 can coconut milk
- Juice of 1 lime
- 1 Tbsp red curry paste
- 1 tsp fish sauce
- 1 tsp coconut aminos
- 1 tsp date paste
- 2 tsp Siracha
- 2 garlic cloves, minced
- 1 tsp ground turmeric
- 1 tsp ground ginger
- ½ tsp sea salt
- ½ tsp white pepper
- 1 pound sea bass/cod, cut into 1-inch cubes
- Garnish: Fresh cilantro, lime wedges

Directions

1. In a large bowl, combine coconut milk, lime juice, red curry paste, fish sauce, date paste, coconut aminos, siracha, ginger, turmeric, white pepper, sea salt. Whisk.
2. Place sea bass/cod in the bottom of instant pot.
3. Pour coconut milk mix over the fish.
4. Lock the lid. Cook on HIGH pressure 5 minutes.
5. Once done, release pressure quickly.
6. Serve fish in bowls. Garnish with cilantro, lime wedges.

Nutrition Value (Per Serving)

Calories: 427

Fat: 20g

Carbohydrates: 28g

Protein: 36g

Cod

(Prep time: 10 minutes\ Cook time: 5 minutes\ 4 servings)

Ingredients

- 4 fresh cod fillets
- 3 Tbsp clarified butter
- Juice of 1 lemon
- 1 onion, diced
- 1 tsp of salt
- ½ tsp black pepper
- 1 tsp oregano
- 1 can (28 oz) diced tomatoes
- Garnish: fresh lemon wedge, parsley

Directions

1. Set instant pot to Sauté. Heat the clarified butter. Sauté onion 2 minutes.
2. Place fish in instant pot. Coat fish in butter. Add rest of ingredients.
3. Lock the lid. Cook on HIGH pressure 5 minutes.
4. Once done, quickly release pressure.
5. Serve on plates. Garnish with parsley, lemon wedge.

Nutrition Value (Per Serving)

Calories: 301
Fat: 14g
Carbohydrates: 14g
Protein: 47g

Sock Eye Salmon

(Prep time: 5 minutes\ Cook time: 5 minutes\ 4 servings)

Ingredients

- 4 Alaskan sockeye salmon fillets
- 1 cup water
- 2 lemons, sliced
- Pinch of salt and pepper
- Garnish: green onions

Directions

1. Add steamer basket to instant pot. Season fillets with salt and pepper.
2. Place fish on steamer basket. Place lime slices on fillets.
3. Lock the lid. Cook on HIGH pressure 5 minutes.
4. Serve. Garnish with sliced green onions.

Nutrition Value (Per Serving)

Calories: 487
Fat: 20g
Carbohydrates: 0g
Protein: 77g

Bowl Of Shrimp

(Prep time: 5 minutes\ Cook time: 5 minutes\ 4 servings)

Ingredients

- 2 pounds shrimp
- 2 Tbsp coconut oil
- 1 Tbsp minced garlic
- ½ cup white grape juice
- ½ cup vegetable broth
- 1 Tbsp lemon juice
- Pinch of salt and pepper
- Garnish: fresh parsley

Directions

1. Set instant pot to Sauté. Heat the coconut oil. Sauté the garlic 1 minute.
2. Add grape juice, vegetable broth to deglaze pot.
3. Add shrimp to pot.
4. Lock the lid. Cook on MEAT/STEW pressure 4 minute.
5. Once done, release pressure naturally.
6. Open the lid. Stir in lemon juice. Season with salt and pepper.
7. Serve hot.

Nutrition Value (Per Serving)

Calories: 181
Fat: 12g

Carbohydrates: 2g
Protein: 16g

Shrimp Chowder

(Prep time: 10 minutes\ Cook time: 17 minutes\ 6 servings)

Ingredients

- 2 Tbsp coconut oil
- 3 large potatoes, peeled, cubed
- 1 large onion
- 2 shallots
- 2 celery stalks, diced
- Zest of 1 lemon
- 1 bay leaf
- 3 cups shrimp or vegetable broth
- 2 cups almond milk
- ½ cup cashew cream
- 2 Tbsp flour
- 1½ pounds fresh shrimp
- Pinch of white pepper
- Pinch of salt and pepper
- Garnish: fresh basil, oyster crackers

Directions

1. Set instant pot to Sauté. Heat the coconut oil. Sauté the onion, shallots 2 minutes. Add the potatoes, bell pepper, and celery.

2. Stir in broth. Add lemon zest, bay leaf
3. Lock the lid. Cook on HIGH pressure 5 minutes.
4. Once done, release pressure naturally.
5. Add the shrimp. Lock the lid. Cook on HIGH pressure 5 minutes.
6. Once done, release pressure naturally.
7. Discard the bay leaf. Using a fork, mash the potatoes to a chunky texture.
8. Set to Sauté. Whisk in cashew cream and milk. Season with white pepper. Simmer 5 minutes.
9. Serve in bowls. Garnish with fresh basil, oyster crackers.

Nutrition Value (Per Serving)

Calories: 590
Fat: 30g

Carbohydrates: 30g
Protein: 51g

Lemon Pepper Salmon

(Prep time: 5 minutes\ Cook time: 10 minutes\ 3-4 servings)

Ingredients

- ¾ cup water
- Few sprigs of parsley, basil, tarragon, basil
- 1 pound salmon, skin on
- 3 tsp ghee
- ¼ tsp salt
- 1 tsp fresh ground black pepper
- ½ fresh lemon, thinly sliced
- 1 red bell pepper, julienned
- 1 carrot, julienned
- Garnish: fresh dill

Directions

1. Set instant pot to Sauté. Pour water into pot. Add the herbs.
2. Place a steamer rack in pot. Place the salmon on the steamer rack.
3. Drizzle ghee over salmon. Season with salt and pepper and salt.
4. Cover with lemon slices.
5. Lock the lid. Cook on HIGH pressure 5 minute.
6. Once done, release pressure naturally.
7. Transfer salmon to serving platter.
8. Add vegetables to instant pot. Set to Sauté. Cook vegetables 5 minutes.

9. Serve with salmon. Garnish with fresh dill.

Nutrition Value (Per Serving)

Calories: 464
Fat: 34g

Carbohydrates: 3g
Protein: 34g

Shrimp Rice

(Prep time: 5 minutes\ Cook time: 5 minutes\ 3-4 servings)

Ingredients

- 2 pounds shrimp
- 2 Tbsp coconut oil
- 1 Tbsp minced garlic
- ½ cup white wine vinegar
- ½ cup vegetable broth
- 1 Tbsp lemon juice
- Pinch of salt and pepper
- Garnish: lemon juice, lemon wedges, fresh parsley
- Cook rice of your choosing; basmati, brown, jasmine to add in dish

Directions

1. Set instant pot to Sauté. Heat the oil. Sauté the garlic 1 minute.
2. Add vinegar and vegetable broth, deglaze the pot. Add the shrimp.
3. Lock the lid. Cook on MEAT/STEW pressure 4 minutes.
4. Once done, release pressure naturally.
5. Open the lid. Add the cooked rice. Season with salt and pepper. Stir.
6. Serve in bowls. Garnish with lemon juice, lemon wedges, fresh parsley.

Nutrition Value (Per Serving)

Calories: 411
Fat: 12g

Carbohydrates: 61g
Protein: 16g

Lobster Bisque

(Prep time: 5 minutes\ Cook time: 15 minutes\ 3-4 servings)

Ingredients

- 4 Lobster tails
- 1 Tbsp coconut oil
- 2 shallots, minced
- 1 garlic clove, minced
- 1 cup carrots, diced
- 1 cup celery, diced
- 1 can (28 oz) diced tomatoes
- 4 cups low sodium vegetable broth
- 1 Tbsp old bay seasoning
- 1 tsp dried dill
- 1 tsp fresh ground black pepper
- 5 tsp paprika
- 1 cup half and half or whipping cream, or your non-dairy choice
- Fresh parsley

Directions

1. Set instant pot to Sauté. Melt the coconut oil. Sauté the garlic, shallots, carrots, celery 5 minutes. Add the tomatoes. Add the old bay seasoning, black pepper, paprika. Stir well.
2. Stir in vegetable broth. Place lobster tails in pot.
3. Lock the lid. Cook on HIGH pressure 5 minutes.
4. Once done, release pressure naturally.
5. Using an immersion blender, pulse a few times to break up lobster and vegetables. You can leave it chunky or pulse to smooth consistency.
6. Set instant pot to Sauté. Stir in half and half, whip cream, or non-dairy. Simmer 5 minutes.
7. Serve in bowls. Garnish with parsley.

Nutrition Value (Per Serving)

Calories: 470
Fat: 25g

Carbohydrates: 20g
Protein: 29g

Country Shrimp

(Prep time: 10 minutes\ Cook time: 10 minutes\ 6 servings)

Ingredients

- 1 large sweet onion, sliced
- 4 garlic cloves, quartered
- 6 medium red potatoes, chopped
- 1 pound frozen, tail-on shrimp
- 1 Tbsp old bay seasoning
- 4 cups vegetable broth
- Juice of 1 lemon.
- 1 lemon, sliced
- Garnish: fresh parsley, fresh ground black pepper

Directions

1. Layer onions along bottom of instant pot. Place garlic over the onions. Add a layer of red potatoes. Place the shrimp on top of the potatoes. Sprinkle old bay seasoning over the ingredients.
2. Slowly pour in the broth. Squeeze lemon over ingredients.
3. Lock the lid. Cook on HIGH pressure 10 minutes.
4. Once done, release pressure quickly.
5. Serve in bowls. Garnish with fresh parsley, ground black pepper

Nutrition Value (Per Serving)

Calories: 317

Fat: 19g

Carbohydrates: 8g

Protein: 3g

Seafood Gumbo

(Prep time: 10 minutes\ Cook time: 6 minutes\ 4 servings)

Ingredients

- 4 sea bass fillets, diced (bite-size pieces)
- 2 pounds medium raw shrimp, make sure they are deveined, tail off
- 3 Tbsp avocado oil
- 3 Tbsp Cajun seasoning
- 2 yellow onion, diced
- 2 bell peppers, diced
- 4 celery stalks, diced
- 1 can (28 oz) diced tomatoes
- ¼ cup tomato paste
- 3 bay leaves
- 1½ cups bone broth
- Pinch of sea salt, fresh ground black pepper
- Garnish: fresh parsley

Directions

1. In a small bowl, combine the Cajun seasoning, salt, pepper. Coat diced fillets and shrimp with seasoning mix.
2. Set instant pot to Sauté. Heat the avocado oil. Sauté onion, garlic, peppers, celery 5 minutes. Add fish chunks and shrimp. Saute 1 minute to let the fish absorb seasoning and create a slightly brown crust.
3. Transfer fish and shrimp to a platter.
4. Stir in diced tomatoes, tomato paste, bay leaves. Pour in the broth slowly.
5. Return fillets and shrimp to instant pot.
6. Lock the lid. Cook on HIGH pressure 5 minutes.
7. Once done, release the pressure naturally. Remove bay leaves.
8. Serve in bowls. Garnish with fresh parsley.

Nutrition Value (Per Serving)

Calories: 460
Fat: 26g

Carbohydrates: 29g
Protein: 29g

Garlic Mussels

(Prep time: 15 minutes\ Cook time: 5 minutes\ 4 servings)

Ingredients

- 3 pounds mussels
- 1 Tbsp extra virgin olive oil
- 4 garlic cloves, minced
- 1 large red bell pepper, diced
- ¾ cup fish broth or vegetable broth
- ½ cup white wine vinegar
- Pinch of red pepper flakes
- 2 Tbsp cashew cream
- Garnish: fresh parsley

Directions

1. Clean the mussels well.
2. Set instant pot to Sauté. Heat the olive oil. Sauté the onion, garlic 3 minutes.
3. Add red pepper, vinegar, fish stock, red pepper flakes, cashew cream. Stir.
4. Add mussels to instant pot. Pour in broth.
5. Lock the lid. Cook on HIGH pressure 2 minutes.
6. Once done, release pressure quickly.
7. Open the lid, check all the mussels are open. If not, lock the lid, steam 1 minute.
8. Serve in bowls. Garnish with fresh parsley.

Nutrition Value (Per Serving)

Calories: 199
Fat: 8g

Carbohydrates: 10g
Protein: 21g

Seafood Stew

(Prep time: 10 minutes\ Cook time: 15 minutes\ 4 servings)

Ingredients

- 2 Tbsp extra-virgin olive oil
- 1 small onion, sliced
- 2 garlic cloves, smashed
- 1 green pepper, sliced
- 1 small can diced tomatoes
- 2 bay leaves
- 2 tsp paprika
- Pinch of sea salt, fresh ground black pepper
- 1 cup fish broth or vegetable broth
- 1½ pounds white fish, cod, halibut, haddock
- 1 pound shrimp, deveined, detailed
- 12 clams
- Garnish: lemon slices, fresh cilantro

Directions

1. Set instant pot to Sauté. Heat the olive oil. Sauté onion, garlic, green pepper 5 minutes. Stir in diced tomatoes.
2. Season with paprika, salt, pepper.
3. Nestle clams, shrimp, white fish on top.
4. Pour in the broth. Add the bay leaves.
5. Lock the lid. Cook on HIGH pressure 10 minutes.
6. Once done, release pressure naturally. Remove bay leaves.
7. Serve in bowls. Garnish with lemon slices, fresh cilantro.

Nutrition Value (Per Serving)

Calories: 401
Fat: 20g
Carbohydrates: 41g
Protein: 41g

Chapter 9: Salads

Beet Salad

(Prep time: 35 minutes\ Cook time: 3 minutes\ 6 servings)

Ingredients

- 6 medium beets, scrubbed, sliced
- Pinch of kosher salt, fresh ground black pepper
- 1 cup water
- Splash of balsamic vinegar
- Garnish: extra virgin olive oil

Directions

1. Wash beets thoroughly. Add water to instant pot.
2. Place steamer/trivet in instant pot. Arrange beets in steamer.
3. Lock the lid. Cook on HIGH pressure 3 minutes.
4. Once done, release pressure naturally. Allow beets to cool.
5. Slice off skin. Slice beets ½-inch slices. Season with salt and pepper.
6. Add splash of balsamic vinegar. Allow to marinate 30 minutes.
7. Serve on a plate. Drizzle with extra virgin olive oil.

Nutrition Value (Per Serving)

Calories: 120   Fat: 7g   Carbohydrates: 13g   Protein: 2g

Kale and Carrots Medley

(Prep time: 5 minutes\ Cook time: 5 minutes\ 8 servings)

Ingredients

- 1 cup kale, stem removed, chopped
- 1 Tbsp olive oil
- 1 medium onion, thinly sliced
- 3 medium carrots, sliced
- 5 garlic cloves, minced
- ½ cup vegetable broth
- Pinch of kosher salt, fresh ground black pepper
- Aged balsamic vinegar
- ¼ tsp red pepper flakes

Directions

1. Set instant pot to Sauté. Heat the olive oil. Sauté onion, garlic, carrots 5 minutes.
2. Pile in the kale. Pour in vegetable broth. Season with salt and pepper.

3. Lock the lid. Cook on HIGH pressure 5 minutes.
4. Once done, release pressure naturally. Stir ingredients.
5. Serve on a platter. Garnish with balsamic vinegar, sprinkle red pepper flakes.

Nutrition Value (Per Serving)

Calories: 223   Fat: 14g   Carbohydrates: 21g   Protein: 10g

Vegetable Salad

(Prep time: 5 minutes\ Cook time: 10 minutes \For 2 servings)

Ingredients

- 1 pound raw almonds
- 2 medium tomatoes, diced
- ½ cup green peppers, diced
- ½ cup broccoli florets
- ½ cup sweet onion, diced
- ¼ cup hot peppers, diced
- ¼ cup celery, diced
- ¾ tsp salt
- ¼ tsp fresh ground black pepper
- Dressing: 2 Tbsp olive oil, 1 Tbsp mustard, juice from ½ lemon, ¼ cup red wine vinegar, pinch of salt, fresh ground pepper. Whisk together.

Directions

1. Add almonds to instant pot. Pour in water.
2. Lock the lid. Cook on HIGH pressure 10 minutes.
3. Drain the water. Set to Sauté. Return almonds to instant pot. Smash with wooden spoon. Sauté 1 minute. Remove from pot. Cool slightly.
4. In a large bowl, combine diced vegetables. Drizzle in iced up vegetables
5. Serve in bowls. Drizzle dressing over vegetables. Top with almonds.

Nutrition Value (Per Serving)

Calories: 140

Fat: 4g

Carbohydrates: 24g

Protein: 5g

Capers And Beet Salad

(Prep time: 10 minutes\ Cook time: 25 minutes\ 4 servings)

Ingredients

- 1 cup water
- 4 medium beets, snip tops, wash thoroughly
- 2 Tbsp rice wine vinegar
- Bunch of fresh parsley, stems removed
- 1 large garlic clove, minced
- ½ tsp salt
- Pinch fresh ground black pepper
- 1 Tbsp extra virgin olive oil
- 2 Tbsp capers
- Garnish: fresh parsley, fresh ground black pepper

Directions

1. Pour water in instant pot. Place steamer basket in pot.
2. Place beets in steamer basket.
3. Lock the lid. Cook on HIGH pressure 25 minutes.
4. Once done, release the pressure naturally.
5. While they cook, in a small jar and chopped parsley, garlic, olive oil, salt, pepper and capers. Place lid on jar. Shake thoroughly.
6. Once done, release pressure naturally. Check doneness of beets.
7. Run beets under cold water briefly. Peel off skins. Slice beets in circles.
8. Arrange on a platter. Drizzle dressing over beets. Garnish with fresh parsley, fresh ground black pepper.

Nutrition Value (Per Serving)

Calories: 43
Fat: 2.4g

Carbohydrates: 5.4g
Protein: 0.7g

Couscous And Vegetable Medley

(Prep time: 10 minutes\ Cook time: 4 minutes\ 3 servings)

Ingredients

- 1 Tbsp olive oil
- 2 bay leaves
- 1 small onion
- 1 cup carrot, grated
- 1 red pepper, diced
- 1¾ cup couscous
- 1¾ cup water
- 2 tsp salt
- ½ tsp Garam masala
- Garnish: lemon juice, lemon wedge, fresh cilantro

Directions

1. Set instant pot to Sauté. Heat the olive oil. Sauté onion, red pepper, carrots 3 minutes.
2. Stir in couscous, garam masala, water, and salt. Stir.
3. Lock the lid. Cook on HIGH pressure 4 minutes.
4. Once done, release pressure naturally. Remove bay leaves.
5. Fluff with a fork. Serve on a platter. Garnish with lemon juice, lemon wedges, fresh cilantro.

Nutrition Value (Per Serving)

Calories: 91

Fat: 2g

Carbohydrates: 18g

Protein: 3g

Stir Fried Bell Pepper and Potatoes

(Prep time: 15 minutes\ Cook time: 4 minutes\ 2 servings)

Ingredients

- 1 Tbsp olive oil
- 2 red bell peppers, cut in strips
- 4 baby potatoes
- 1 small onion, diced
- 4 garlic cloves, minced
- ½ tsp cumin seeds
- ½ tsp dry mango
- ¼ tsp turmeric
- ½ tsp cayenne
- 2 tsp coriander
- 1 tsp salt
- 2 Tbsp water
- Garnish: fresh cilantro

Directions

1. Set instant pot to Sauté. Heat the olive oil. Sauté onion, garlic, red pepper, baby potatoes.
2. Season with cumin seeds, dry mango, turmeric, cayenne pepper, coriander, salt.
3. Sprinkle water over the ingredients. Stir well.
4. Lock the lid. Cook on HIGH pressure 4 minutes.
5. Once done, release pressure naturally.
6. Stir in mango powder, lemon juice.
7. Serve on platter. Garnish with fresh cilantro.

Nutrition Value (Per Serving)

Calories: 333   Fat: 24g   Carbohydrates: 11g   Protein: 18g

Lentil and Farro Salad

(Prep time: 15 minutes\ Cook time: 12 minutes\ 4 servings)

Ingredients

Lentils

- ½ cup lentils
- 1¼ cup water
- ½ tsp dried oregano
- ½ tsp chili powder
- ½ tsp dried basil
- ½ tsp salt
- ¼ tsp cumin powder
- ¼ tsp smoked paprika
- ¼ tsp onion powder
- ¼ tsp garlic powder
- ¼ tsp black pepper

Farro

- ½ cup faro
- 1 cup water
- ½ tsp Italian herbs
- ½ tsp onion powder
- ½ tsp salt
- Garnish: fresh parsley

Directions

1. Place all the ingredients listed under Lentils in instant pot.
2. Place trivet on top of the lentils.
3. Add faro ingredients to a stainless steel bowl. Place it on top of trivet.
4. Lock the lid. Cook on HIGH pressure 12 minutes.
5. Once done, release the pressure naturally.
6. Combine the ingredients. Serve on a platter. Garnish with fresh parsley.

Nutrition Value (Per Serving)

Calories: 350   Fat: 19g   Carbohydrates: 38g   Protein: 12g

Peruvian Quinoa

(Prep time: 5 minutes\ Cook time: 4 minutes\ 4 servings)

Ingredients

- 1 cup well rinsed quinoa
- Pinch of salt
- Zest and lime of 1 lime
- 1 cup cooked vegetables, your choice
- Garnish: fresh parsley

Directions

1. Add quinoa, zest, water, and salt to instant pot.
2. Lock the lid. Cook on HIGH pressure 4 minutes.
3. Once done, release pressure naturally.
4. Fluff with a fork. Stir in lime juice.
5. Mix with cooked vegetables. Serve on a platter. Garnish with fresh parsley.

Nutrition Value (Per Serving)

Calories: 321

Fat: 5g

Carbohydrates: 38g

Protein: 32g

English Peas And Asparagus

(Prep time: 10 minutes\ Cook time: 4 minutes\ 4 servings)

Ingredients

- 2 garlic cloves, minced
- 2 cups English peas
- 10 asparagus stalks, diced
- ½ cup vegetable broth
- Zest and juice of 1 lemon
- Garnish: pine nuts

Directions

1. Add garlic, asparagus, peas and broth to instant pot.
2. Lock the lid. Cook on LOW pressure 4 minutes.
3. Once done, release pressure quickly.
4. Stir. Add lemon zest and juice and give it a nice stir
5. Transfer to serving platter. Garnish with pine nuts.

Nutrition Value (Per Serving)

Calories: 289

Fat: 18g

Carbohydrates: 6g

Protein: 26g

Cauliflower Citrus Salad

(Prep time: 10 minutes\ Cook time: 7 minutes\ 4 servings)

Ingredients

- 1 small cauliflower, cut in florets
- 1 small romanesco cauliflower, cut in florets
- 1 head broccoli, cut in florets
- 2 seedless oranges, peeled, sliced

Vinaigrette

- Zest and juice of 1 orange
- 4 anchovies
- 1 hot pepper, diced
- 1 Tbsp capers
- 4 Tbsp extra virgin olive oil
- Pinch of salt and pepper

Directions

1. Add broccoli and cauliflower to instant pot. Pour in 1 cup of water.
2. Lock the lid. Cook on HIGH pressure 7 minutes.
3. Make vinaigrette: combine anchovies, capers, hot pepper, olive oil, salt, and pepper. Whisk together to combine fully.
4. Once done, release pressure quickly.
5. Strain the vegetables. Allow to cool slightly.
6. Combine the broccoli, cauliflower in a bowl. Add orange slices. Stir in vinaigrette. Garnish with fresh mint.

Nutrition Value (Per Serving)

Calories: 69

Fat: 4g

Carbohydrates: 8g

Protein: 3g

Egg and Olive Potato Salad

(Prep time: 15 minutes\ Cook time: 12 minutes\ 4 servings)

Ingredients

- 2 cups water
- 3 eggs
- 2 pounds yellow potatoes, cubed
- ½ tsp black pepper
- ½ tsp salt
- ¼ tsp paprika
- Pinch of cayenne pepper
- 4 Tbsp anti-inflammatory compliant mayo
- 2 tsp Dijon mustard
- 4 green olives, sliced
- 2 Tbsp red onion, finely chopped
- 2 celery stalks, diced
- 2 chives, minced

Directions

1. Pour water in instant pot.
2. Place steamer rack in pot. Add potatoes and eggs on top of rack.
3. Lock the lid. Cook on LOW pressure 12 minutes.
4. Once done, release the pressure naturally.
5. Transfer eggs to ice bath. Chop up the eggs. Cool eggs and potatoes.
6. In a bowl, combine the potatoes, eggs, olives, celery, black pepper, salt, paprika, mayonnaise. Stir well to coat the ingredients.
7. Garnish with chopped chives. Chill until ready to consume.

Nutrition Value (Per Serving)

Calories: 301
Fat: 22g
Carbohydrates: 22g
Protein: 4g

Sweet Pickle Potato Salad

(Prep time: 15 minutes\ Cook time: 10 minutes\ 4 servings)

Ingredients

- 1 cup water
- 5 small russet potatoes, peeled, diced
- 3 eggs
- ⅔ cup anti-inflammatory compliant mayo
- 1 Tbsp yellow mustard
- ½ cup sliced mini gherkins pickles, chopped
- ¼ tsp garlic powder
- ¼ tsp onion powder
- Pinch of salt and pepper
- Dash of paprika

Directions

1. Pour water in bottom of instant pot.
2. Place steamer basket in pot. Place potatoes and eggs on basket.
3. Lock the lid. Cook on HIGH pressure 10 minutes.
4. Once done, release pressure quickly.
5. Transfer eggs to cold water. Cool eggs and potatoes.
6. In a bowl, combine eggs, potatoes, chopped pickles, garlic powder, onion powder, salt, and pepper. In a separate bowl, mix the mustard and mayonnaise. Add it to the salad. Mix well. Garnish with paprika.
7. Chill until ready to serve.

Nutrition Value (Per Serving)

Calories: 269
Fat: 12g
Carbohydrates: 37g
Protein: 5g

Quinoa Salad

(Prep time: 10 minutes\ Cook time: 2 minutes\ 4 servings)

Ingredients

- 1 cup quinoa
- 1¼ cup water
- 1½ cup strawberries, sliced
- 1 cup pecans, chopped
- 2 green onions, chopped
- 1 cup broccoli florets, minced

Dressing

- 2 Tbsp balsamic vinegar
- ¼ cup olive oil
- ¼ tsp garlic powder
- 1 Tbsp fresh basil, minced

Directions

1. Add water and quinoa to instant pot.
2. Lock the lid. Cook on HIGH 2 minutes.
3. In a separate bowl, combine the balsamic vinegar, olive oil, garlic powder, green onion, and fresh basil. Whisk to combine.
4. In another bowl, combine the fruit, nuts, vegetables.
5. Once done, release pressure naturally. Fluff the quinoa.
6. Transfer to a large bowl. Add the fruit, nuts, vegetable mixture. Stir in the vinaigrette.
7. Garnish with more fresh basil.

Nutrition Value (Per Serving)

Calories: 156
Fat: 3g

Carbohydrates: 27g
Protein: 6g

Chapter 10: Dessert

Apple Sauce

(Prep time: 15 minutes\ Cook time: 10 minutes\ 2 servings)

Ingredients

- 12 medium red delicious apples, peeled, diced
- Pinch of cinnamon
- ½ cup water
- Garnish: fresh mint

Directions

1. Place peeled apples in instant pot. Pour in the water. Sprinkle cinnamon.
2. Cut a circle piece of parchment paper large enough to fit over the apples.
3. Lock the lid. Cook on HIGH pressure 10 minutes.
4. Once done, release pressure naturally.
5. Remove the parchment paper.
6. Using an immersion blender, pulse until a smooth consistency.
7. Transfer to glass bowls. Garnish with fresh mint.

Nutrition

Calories: 55
Fat: 0g
Carbohydrates: 15g
Protein: 0g

Mango Sticky Rice

(Prep time: 15 minutes\ Cook time: 5 minutes\ 2 servings)

Ingredients

- 1 cup jasmine rice
- 1¼ cup lightly sweetened coconut milk + 1/3 cup
- 1 cup frozen mango chunks
- Garnish: Black sesame seeds

Directions

1. Add jasmine rice and the 1¼ cup lightly sweetened coconut milk to instant pot.
2. Add mango chunks on top.
3. Lock the lid. Cook on HIGH pressure 5 minutes.
4. Once done, release pressure naturally.
5. Fluff the rice. Stir in extra coconut milk.
6. Serve in bowls. Garnish with black sesame seeds.

Nutrition Value (Per Serving)

Calories: 50
Fat: 4.4g

Carbohydrates: 3.1g
Protein: 0.7g

<u>Apple Bake</u>

(Prep time: 15 minutes\ Cook time: 10 minutes\ 5 servings)

Ingredients

- 6 red delicious apples, peeled, diced
- ¼ cup raisins
- 1 cup red wine vinegar
- ½ cup raw demerara sugar
- 1 tsp ground cinnamon

Directions

1. Add apples to instant pot. Pour in red wine vinegar, cinnamon, and raisins.
2. Lock the lid. Cook on HIGH pressure 10 minutes.
3. Once done, release pressure naturally.
4. Serve in bowls. Drizzle cooking liquid over apples.

Nutrition Value (Per Serving)

Calories: 332
Fat: 17g

Carbohydrates: 45g
Protein: 3g

<u>Apple Cranberry</u>

(Prep time: 10 minutes\ Cook time: 12 minutes\ 6 servings)

Ingredients

- 1 cup frozen cranberries
- 1 orange, peeled, sliced
- 1 apple, peeled, chopped
- ½ cup apple cider
- ½ cup maple syrup
- Garnish: fresh mint

Directions

1. Add listed ingredients to instant pot. Stir.
2. Lock the lid. Cook on HIGH pressure 10 minutes.
3. Once done, release pressure naturally.
4. Set pot to Sauté. Simmer 2 minutes.
5. Serve in bowls. Garnish with fresh mint.

Nutrition Value (Per Serving)

- Calories: 110
- Fat: 0g
- Carbohydrates: 26g
- Protein: 1g

Carrot Puree

(Prep time: 15 minutes\ Cook time: 10 minutes\ 5 servings)

Ingredients

- 1½ pound carrots, chopped small
- 1 Tbsp coconut oil
- 1 Tbsp honey
- ¼ tsp sea salt
- 1 cup water
- Garnish: fresh mint

Directions

1. Pour water in instant pot.
2. Set steamer rack in pot. Place carrots in rack.
3. Lock the lid. Cook on HIGH pressure 10 minutes.
4. Once done, release pressure quickly.
5. Set instant pot to Sauté. Add the coconut oil, honey, sea salt to pot.
6. Using an immersion blender, pulse until smooth consistency.
7. Transfer to serving bowl. Garnish with fresh mint.

Nutrition Value (Per Serving)

Calories: 143
Fat: 9g

Carbohydrates: 16g
Protein: 2g

Cranberry Sauce

(Prep time: 15 minutes\ Cook time: 10 minutes\ 2-4 servings)

Ingredients

- 1 cup cranberries
- 2½ tsp orange zest
- ¼ cup fresh squeezed orange juice
- 2 Tbsp maple syrup
- Pinch of salt

Directions

1. Place cranberries, maple syrup, orange juice and zest to instant pot. Stir.
2. Lock the lid. Cook on HIGH pressure 10 minutes.
3. Once done, release pressure naturally. Stir.

4. Using an immersion blender, pulse until smooth consistency.
5. Transfer to glass dish. Chill unused portion.

Nutrition Value (Per Serving)

Calories: 176 Carbohydrates: 41g
Fat: 0g Protein: 0g

Gaja Ka Halwa (Pudding - India)

(Prep time: 10 minutes\ Cook time: 15 minutes\ 10 servings)

Ingredients

- 6 medium sweet potatoes, peeled, halved
- 1 cup almond milk
- 4 green cardamoms (slightly bruised)
- ½ cup green raisins
- ¼ cup coconut oil
- Garnish: slivered almonds, dried rose petals, crushed

Directions

1. Place sweet potatoes in bottom of instant pot.
2. Add almond milk, cardamoms, raisins, and brown sugar. Stir.
3. Lock the lid. Cook on HIGH pressure 10 minutes.
4. Once done, release pressure naturally.
5. Remove the cardamoms. Mash the potatoes.
6. Add raisins.
7. Set to Sauté. Add the coconut oil. Simmer 5 minutes.
8. Serve in a dish. Garnish with slivered almonds and rose petals.

Nutrition Value (Per Serving)

Calories: 300 Carbohydrates: 42g
Fat: 12g Protein: 7g

Conclusion

I would like to thank you again for purchasing the book and taking the time for going through the book as well.

I do hope this book was insightful and you found the information useful!

Keep in mind that you are not only limited to the recipes provided in this book. Continue to explore and experiment with healthy eating. The possibilities are endless.

Stay healthy and stay safe!

Made in the USA
Middletown, DE
01 October 2018